The West

An Illustrated History
for Children

Based on the Public Television Series

THE WEST

The West

An Illustrated History for Children

•· ·•· ·•·

by Dayton Duncan

With an Introduction by Stephen Ives and Ken Burns

Little, Brown and Company

BOSTON   NEW YORK   TORONTO   LONDON

For Emmy, my inquisitive daughter,

whose questions helped me write this book

•◆• •◆• •◆•

First Edition

Photography credits appear on page 136.

Library of Congress Cataloging-in-Publication Data

Duncan, Dayton.
    The West : an illustrated history for children / by Dayton Duncan ;
  with an introduction by Stephen Ives and Ken Burns.—1st ed.
      p. cm.
  Includes bibliographical references and index.
  Summary: A presentation, based on a PBS television documentary, of the story of the West, a magnificent but harsh landscape, and the people who have tried to claim it.
  ISBN 0-316-19628-2 (hc)
  ISBN 0-316-19632-0 (pb)
    1. West (U.S.)—History—Juvenile literature.   [1. West (U.S.)—
History.] I. Title.
   F591.D844 1996
   978—dc20   95-26722

10 9 8 7 6 5 4 3 2 1

Q-KP

Published simultaneously in Canada by Little, Brown & Company (Canada) Limited
and in Great Britain by Little, Brown and Company (UK) Limited

Printed in the United States of America

Contents

Introduction

The West stretches from the Mississippi River to the Pacific Ocean, from the northern plains to the Rio Grande—more than two million square miles of the most extraordinary landscape on earth.

It is a land of grasslands and deserts and mountain barriers: the Rockies and Wasatch, the Bitterroots and Bighorns, the Sierra Nevada and Sangre de Cristo, the Confusions, the Crazies, and the Black Hills.

It is a land of rivers: the Colorado and Columbia and Missouri, the Sweetwater and the Platte, Sand Creek and the Greasy Grass, the River that Scolds All Others, and the River of No Return.

The West is a land of infinite horizons and unimaginable distances. But it was never empty. To the Native Americans it was home, the center of the universe. To the Spanish, who came from their colony of Mexico, it was the north. The British and French arrived by coming south, out of Canada, while the Chinese and Russians came by sailing east. But it was the Americans—the last to arrive—who named it the West and then made it part of their nation.

Like the television series upon which it is based, this book tells the story of the West—of a magnificent but harsh landscape and the many people who have tried to claim it. It is a story of conquest, of colliding ideals, of competing promises and competing visions of the land. It is a story of dreams and myths, of hopes fulfilled and hopes denied.

The history of the West is filled with both the famous and the little known. We have tried to include a sampling of each. Likewise, we have touched on some of the most dramatic triumphs in the history of the West—as well as the human price paid for each success.

No book or film could ever tell the whole story. But we hope that our telling suggests the broad outlines of the rich and complicated history of the West, in all its dizzying variety and conflicting emotions. We have filled in those outlines with the personal stories of memorable westerners. Their lives help us understand not only the individuals themselves but also the time and place in which they lived.

We also hope that after reading this introduction to the West, you will seek to fill in its outlines on your own. The West's story never ends—and it always needs more explorers.

—Stephen Ives and Ken Burns

The People
Through 1805

For a thousand generations, the West belonged only to Native Americans. There were perhaps three million of them, living in more than two hundred tribes and speaking more than seventy-five different languages. Each tribe had its own name—the Kalispel and Clatsop and Tonkawa; the Hopi, Mojave, Paiute, and Pawnee; the Dineh and Nimipu; and many more.

Each tribe also had its own story about how it came to exist, a story that usually linked its people to the land itself. The Comanches said they came from swirls of dust, the Hidatsas from the bottom of a big lake. The Nimipu believed that a special being named Coyote once defeated a giant monster along the Clearwater River, and on the spot where the monster's blood mixed with river water and earth, their ancestors sprang up. Among

Crow girls and their dogs

A Kwakiutl chief from the Pacific Northwest

the sacred bundles of the Zuñis was a stone, they said, within which beats the heart of the world.

There were people who lived in large houses made from the tallest trees on earth and people who lived in isolated huts made from branches and twigs. Some lived in tepees covered with animal skins and moved from place to place, following buffalo herds on foot and using dogs to carry their few belongings. Others built permanent cities, with adobe houses several stories high or round lodges made of dirt.

Their customs were as varied as their dwellings and languages. In some tribes, war was considered the most important undertaking and a family's wealth was measured in slaves. In others, women owned all the property and when two people married, the husband moved in with the wife's family. Some started prairie fires to make pastures or dammed streams to irrigate their crops.

Others considered the earth their mother, dared not alter its surface, and prayed to the spirits of the animals they hunted.

They were all different, and yet they were connected. In every direction and in every corner of the West were trails, worn down over the centuries by the comings and goings of tribes trading with one another. Ocean shells from the Pacific coast passed along the trails as a kind of money exchanged for goods, ending up as decorations worn by people who lived east of the Great Plains, thousands of miles from the western sea. Buffalo robes warmed people who had never seen a buffalo. And cornmeal was eaten by people who had never planted corn. People who worshiped different gods, inhabited entirely different worlds, and were sometimes unaware of each other's existence were linked by trade.

They were linked in another respect as well. The special name each tribe had for itself most often translated simply as "the people." But after Christopher Columbus landed in the New World in 1492, newcomers began arriving who gave "the people" a new name that lumped them all together: Indians. The newcomers would do more than just change "the people's" names. They would change the West, and the lives of its first inhabitants, forever.

▪◆▪ ▪◆▪ ▪◆▪

Coyote took blood from a monster's heart, mixed it with water from the river, and sprinkled it on the land. "This," he said, "will be my greatest creation. You will be the Nimipu, the real people."

—*Nez Percé creation story*

Cheyenne men, painted for a sun dance ceremony

In the summer of 1540, in what is now New Mexico, the Zuñis looked down from their mesa-top pueblo named Hawikuh and saw a strange sight. Approaching from the desert to the south was a caravan of more than a thousand people. Most of them were Indians, but there were also several hundred men carrying long lances, wearing metal helmets and breastplates that glistened in the sun, and riding monstrous animals no western Indian had ever seen before—horses.

The caravan was led by Francisco Vásquez de Coronado, who had traveled north from Mexico on behalf of the king of Spain, pursuing rumors of tremendous treasure said to exist in the fabled Seven Cities of Gold. Four years earlier, Alvar Núñez Cabeza de Vaca, the first European to reach the West, had reported that Indians he met spoke of "populous towns...and many turquoise stones" farther to the north than he had gone, though he had never seen any himself. Based on that slim evidence, Coronado had been sent to find the cities, claim their wealth and lands for Spain, and begin converting their people to Christianity.

The Zuñi warriors went down to find out what the strangers wanted. Through an interpreter, Coronado told them that he was on a sacred mission. If they did not peacefully submit to the Spanish soldiers and priests,

Coronado and his conquistadors

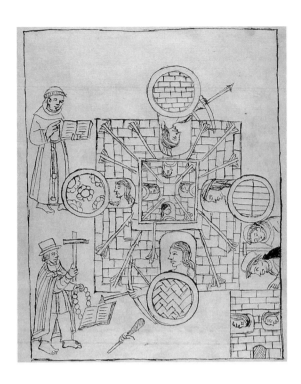

The attack on the Zuñis,
as imagined by
a European artist

he warned, "we shall...do to you all the harm and damage that we can." The Zuñis answered by hurling stones and shooting arrows. Coronado himself was knocked twice from his horse, but in the end, the Zuñis were overpowered by the Spanish horses, lances, and guns, whose thunderous sound they had never heard before.

Coronado's men took over Hawikuh, seized the Indians' food for themselves, and set up a wooden cross, demanding that the Zuñis pray before it. But they found no gold or silver.

Coronado refused to abandon his quest for the Seven Cities of Gold and sent expeditions to explore the surrounding countryside. One group marched southwest to the Gulf of California. Another crossed the Painted Desert into the land of the Hopi and what is now Arizona. And a third came to the edge of a great gorge, whose size was beyond anything the Europeans had ever imagined—the Grand Canyon. Still, there was no treasure.

In the spring of 1541, Coronado led another expedition, chasing yet another myth. Farther north, rumors said, was a place called Quivira, where trees were decorated by golden bells and everyone used plates and cups made of silver and gold. He left the pueblos and headed northeast

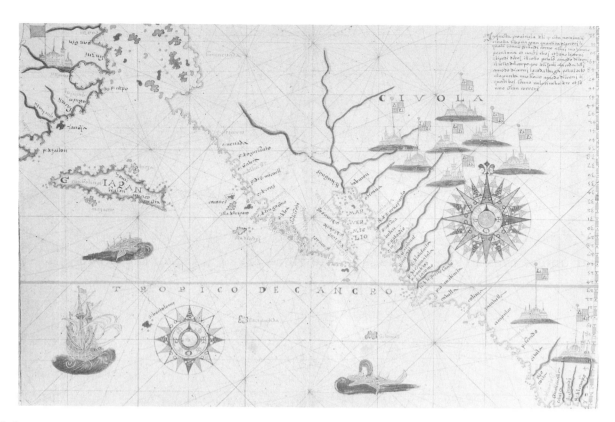

Although no one had ever seen them, the Seven Cities of Gold appeared on European maps.

onto the Great Plains. The vast, treeless expanses were as astonishing to the white men as the Grand Canyon had been. "Who could believe," one wrote, "that 1,000 horses and 500 of our cows and more than 5,000 rams and ewes and more than 1,500 friendly Indians and servants, in traveling over these plains, would leave no more trace when they had passed than if nothing had been there—nothing."

The Europeans were equally surprised and fascinated by the huge herds of buffalo that blanketed the prairies. But when they reached Quivira (in what is now Kansas), it turned out to be just a cluster of huts surrounded by bean fields. Its inhabitants were no wealthier than the other Indians they had encountered.

The country itself is the best I have ever seen for producing all the products of Spain.... But what I am sure of is that there is not any gold.

—*Francisco Vásquez de Coronado*

Coronado ordered his exhausted and disappointed men to begin the long march back to Mexico. "I have done all that I possibly could," he wrote to the king of Spain, "to discover a country where God Our

Lord might be served and the royal [treasury] increased." He had failed at both.

His search pursuing the myth of the Seven Cities of Gold had lasted three years and led him across a quarter of the West. But his quest had earned him and Spain nothing—except the hatred and fear of the native people they had met along the way.

In 1598, half a century after Coronado's failure, the Spanish returned to the West. The old tales of treasure still lured them, but they also worried that unless they colonized the lands north of Mexico, other European nations would crowd in. In addition, they believed that it was their religious duty to convert the Indians and thereby "save" their souls, even if it sometimes required killing those who resisted.

Soon, thousands of Indians had been baptized by Spanish missionaries, although many still held on to their old beliefs and practices. Every pueblo, or settlement, in the new Spanish province of New Mexico had its own mission church, built by Indian hands. Priests taught their "converts" how to tend herds of sheep and cattle and to grow crops of wheat, apples,

The mission church
at a Zuñi pueblo

plums, and oranges. Wealthy colonists established haciendas, Spanish-style plantations, and used Indian labor, just as Spanish lords relied on serfs in Spain. Soldiers enforced the new system and protected the pueblos from enemy tribes, such as the Navajos and Apaches, who periodically raided them for food, horses, and captives. In 1609—roughly the same time that the French founded Quebec in Canada and the English settled Jamestown on the Atlantic coast—a new capital near the Rio Grande was established for the Spanish colony. It was called Santa Fe— the city of "Holy Faith."

But by 1680—nearly a century before the thirteen American colonies became independent of England—a rebellion was already brewing among the Indians of the West. European diseases had killed a third of the Pueblo Indians. Summer after summer, it had refused to rain. With the drought came famine, and more raids from the Navajos and Apaches. A Tewa medicine man called Popé began preaching that the misfortunes had arrived because the ancient spirits were displeased. They would be satisfied, he said, only when the foreigners were driven out and the people could practice the religion of their choice.

Hopis perform a ceremonial snake dance.

The Spanish priests redoubled their efforts to eliminate the Pueblo Indians' traditional faith. Ritual dances were forbidden and religious relics burned. Twice, Popé was flogged publicly, but he could not be silenced. He sent messages from pueblo to pueblo, urging the people to set aside their ancient differences, band together, and fight for freedom.

On August 10, 1680, the pueblos across northern New Mexico rebelled. Twenty-one of the thirty-three priests in the colony were killed, along with 375 Spanish settlers and their servants. Mission churches were burned to the ground. At Santa Fe, terrified colonists and their allies huddled inside the Palace of the Governors. More than two thousand Pueblo warriors surrounded them, cut off their water, burned the rest of the capital, and sang Catholic hymns in Latin to mock their captives.

After eleven days of siege, the Indians finally let the surviving Spaniards leave for the mission of El Paso, far to the south. It was enough that the land was theirs and theirs alone once more.

Popé had led the most successful Indian revolt in North American history. But his victory would not last long.

According to Cheyenne traditions, there was once a prophet named Sweet Medicine. He taught his people many things—how chiefs should be selected, what rituals to follow in special ceremonies, and how to use four sacred arrows for success in war and hunting. He also predicted the future.

Someday, he said, the Cheyenne would see a new animal. It would have a shaggy neck, round hooves, and a long tail almost touching the ground. Sweet Medicine continued:

> *This animal will carry you on his back and help you in many ways. Those far hills that seem only a blue vision in the distance take many days to reach now. But with this animal, you can get there in a short time, so fear him not.*
>
> *—Sweet Medicine*

"This animal will carry you on his back and help you in many ways. Those far hills that seem only a blue vision in the distance take many days to reach now. But with this animal, you can get there in a short time, so fear him not." The animal was the horse—and it would revolutionize the lives of the Cheyenne, and that of every other Indian people.

European horses quickly spread throughout the West.

Apache and Navajo warriors acquired horses first, from their raids on Spanish settlements. But after the Spanish were driven out of New Mexico, the big herds of horses they left behind spread across the West and were traded from one tribe to the next. By the early 1700s, virtually every tribe had them.

Few tribes were more transformed by the horse than the Cheyenne. They had been a farming people, living in permanent villages in what is now Minnesota, until their enemies, the Lakotas (also called the Sioux), began pushing them westward. They tended crops and sometimes ventured onto the edges of the Great Plains to hunt buffalo—a difficult task on foot.

But with the arrival of the horse, suddenly a mounted warrior could kill enough buffalo in a day to feed and clothe his family for months. A horse could carry and pull much greater weights than a dog was able to, and it could travel much faster. Families could now transport larger tepees and more belongings and food, and they could travel much farther. Soon, the Cheyenne abandoned farming entirely and began following the buffalo herds deeper into the Great Plains.

Many other tribes did the same. The plains became a crowded meeting ground for nearly thirty tribes that moved in from every direction. For the Cheyenne and others, the horse became the symbol of wealth and prestige—a faster way to reach one's enemies and a valuable prize to steal from them. A man's bravery was measured by the size of his horse herd and by the number of times he had touched an enemy in battle—called "counting coup." "When our enemies were not bothering us," a Crow woman named Pretty-Shield remembered, "our warriors were bothering them, so there was always fighting going on somewhere. We women sometimes tried to keep our men from going to war, but this was like talking to winter winds."

Even though many tribes had yet to meet a European, other signs of the white man began to appear. Guns and manufactured goods made their way over the trading trails, giving some tribes advantages over others.

The horse transformed the lives of many Indians.

But if some tribes were strengthened by the horse and the gun, all were threatened by something else brought to America by the far-off strangers—disease. Smallpox, cholera, tuberculosis, measles, and other European diseases against which the Indians had no immunity raced from people to people. Sicknesses spread throughout the West far in advance of the whites who originally carried the diseases. In 1782, smallpox reached the Blackfeet on the northern plains, killing perhaps half of their people. Then it crossed over the Bitterroot Mountains and killed half of the Nez Percés—a quarter of a century before they would even see a white man.

Throughout the 1700s, the monarchs of Europe competed with one another to add the West to their empires—even though few whites had yet been there.

French explorers sailed down the Mississippi River and claimed the land watered by its tributaries, all the way to the Rocky Mountains. In honor of King Louis XIV, they named the vast territory Louisiana.

British fur traders probed south from Hudson's Bay in Canada, seeking wealth from Indian tribes on the far northern plains, and English ships sailed along the northern Pacific coast to exchange manufactured goods for sea otter pelts. The Russians set up outposts on the shores of what is now Alaska and began looking farther south to extend their trading network.

And less than twenty years after Popé's revolt, Spain reconquered New Mexico, then sent soldiers and priests north to colonize the coast of California. They founded twenty-one Catholic missions from San Diego to San Francisco and often forced neighboring tribes to construct the mission buildings, labor in the fields, and convert to Christianity. Within fifty years, three out of every four coastal Indians died from disease, malnutrition, and mistreatment. Near the Mission San Gabriel in southern California, where earthquake tremors were so strong that the Spanish were shaken off their feet, forty-six settlers built a town. It was called El Pueblo de Nuestra Señora la Reina de los Angeles—the Town of Our Lady, the Queen of the Angels—and it would one day become the biggest city in the West.

By 1800, the West had been encircled. But the vast interior was still a great mystery, a blank on the map to the foreign powers. All considered it a great prize waiting to be taken, for there were still rumors of fabulous treasure yet to be found. And there were other myths as well—of woolly mammoths roaming the plains, of erupting volcanoes and mountains made of pure salt, even of a tribe of blue-eyed, red-haired Indians who spoke Welsh.

As this map shows, in the late 1700s, much of the West was still largely unexplored and unknown by whites.

But of all the myths about the West that spurred the Europeans on, the most powerful and longest lasting was that of a fabled Northwest Passage. According to this myth, the western mountains were no bigger or broader than those in the East. Through those mountains, white people believed, ran a river that would link the Atlantic and Pacific Oceans. This river passage would make travel and trade between Europe and Asia much easier—and far more profitable.

Everyone agreed that the nation that discovered the

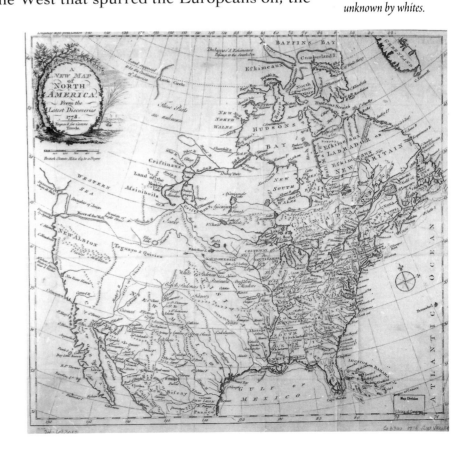

Northwest Passage, and then controlled its traffic, would dominate the entire continent. The West was the prize. The Northwest Passage was seen as the key to winning it.

Now a young republic on the Atlantic seaboard would enter the international race to find it.

No Indian people were more accustomed to the comings and goings of Europeans than the Mandans of the upper Missouri River, successful farmers in what is now North Dakota. For generations, tribes from all over the Great Plains had traveled to the Mandans' permanent villages to exchange meat, hides, horses, and guns for their corn, squash, and beans.

At different times, French, English, and Spanish traders had also visited. Each time, the Europeans brought flags and claimed that the Mandans and their land had now been added to their nation's empire. The Mandans, however, believed that they had merely added the French, English, and Spanish to their long list of customers. By 1804, some 4,500

Mandan earth lodges were big enough for large families — and their prized horses.

people lived in the villages of the Mandans and their allies, the Hidatsas — more than lived in St. Louis or Washington, D.C., at the time.

Then, on October 24, the Mandans looked down the river; coming toward them was the largest boat they had ever seen. It was fifty-five feet long with a tall mast at its center and had twenty-two oars along its sides, a cannon mounted in front, and a small red, white, and blue flag fluttering above. A group of nearly forty-five men stepped on shore, and the Mandans hurried down to greet them.

*T*he object of your mission is to explore the Missouri River [for] the most direct and practicable water communication across this continent.

— *Thomas Jefferson's instructions to Lewis and Clark*

The strangers' two leaders distributed gifts, then proclaimed that the Mandans' old European "fathers" had gone home "beyond the great lake toward the rising sun" and would never return. They had been replaced by a new "great father," more powerful than the others before him, "who could consume you as the fire consumes the grass of the plains." But this new father wanted peace, not war, they said, and under his leadership and protection, the Mandans — and all his Indian "children" — would prosper.

The new "great father" was Thomas Jefferson, president of the United States. A year earlier, he had purchased from France the vast Louisiana Territory. For fifteen million dollars, he bought more than five hundred million acres between the Mississippi River and the Rocky Mountains, more than doubling the size of his country with a single stroke of the pen.

Jefferson had sent what he called his Corps of Discovery to explore the Louisiana Territory, to inform the Indians of the new American claim on their lands, and, most important, to find the fabled Northwest Passage and reach the Pacific Ocean. Locating the Northwest Passage was so important to Jefferson that he had actually planned the expedition before he purchased the new territory.

The expedition's two leaders were Meriwether Lewis and William Clark. With them were young men from Kentucky, Virginia, Pennsylvania, and New Hampshire; two soldiers who had Indian mothers and white fathers; French-Canadian boatmen; and Clark's slave, a black man named York. Lewis also brought along a big Newfoundland dog.

Meriwether Lewis

The explorers spent the winter with the Mandans, who supplied them with corn, helped them hunt buffalo, and told the captains what to expect farther west.

In April of 1805, Lewis and Clark sent their big boat back with a small crew to St. Louis, loaded down with scientific specimens for President Jefferson: antelope skins, coyote bones, Indian bows and arrows, painted buffalo robes, corn—and wooden cages holding a live grouse, four magpies, and a prairie dog.

Then Lewis and Clark said good-bye to the Mandans and headed in the opposite direction, traveling in canoes toward the upper reaches of the Missouri River, the elusive Northwest Passage, and places, Lewis wrote, "on which the foot of civilized man had never trodden."

There were thirty-three members of the expedition now, including three new travelers brought along from the Mandan villages. To act as translators with the Indians they expected to meet, the captains had hired Touissant Charbonneau, a French fur trader, and one of his Indian wives, a sixteen-year-old Shoshone named Sacagawea (Bird Woman), who had been captured by the Hidatsas as a small girl. With them was their infant son, Jean Baptiste.

But for the next four months, as the Corps of Discovery crossed what is now Montana, there was no translating to do. They met no Indians. The only people they saw were each other.

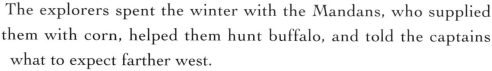

The number of animals along the river, however, astonished them all. Beavers swam near the boats, and Lewis's dog dove in to retrieve one; later, he caught an antelope in the river. Elk, deer, bighorn sheep, coyotes, wolves, and eagles became common sights. Clark estimated that from one hilltop, he could see ten thousand buffalo blanketing the plains. "The game is getting so plenty and tame," one expedition member wrote, "that some of the men has went up near enough to club them out of their way."

By early August they finally neared the mountains and the headwaters of the Missouri. Lewis led a small advance party ahead, hoping to find the Northwest Passage, the goal of explorers for the last three centuries. On

William Clark

Elk and buffalo were common sights during the trip west.

August 12, he climbed toward a gentle ridge. It was the Continental Divide, beyond which rivers run to the Pacific. On the other side, Lewis thought, there would be a great plain with a big river flowing toward the sea.

Instead, as far as his eyes could see were more mountains. And their tops were already partially covered with snow. Like so many other stories and rumors that had spread about the West, the Northwest Passage turned out to be just a myth.

The game is getting so plenty and tame in this country that some of the men has went up near enough to club them out of their way.

—*Private Joseph Whitehouse, Lewis and Clark expedition*

Lewis had no time to rest. The big mountains looming in the distance had to be crossed before winter snows trapped the expedition. They needed horses now, not boats. In what is now Idaho, he finally came upon a band of Shoshones with large horse herds. The Shoshones had never seen a white man before and were suspicious of Lewis's intentions. The

*An artist's conception of
Lewis and Clark,
with York and Sacagawea*

fate of the expedition now lay in their hands.

Then occurred one of the greatest coincidences in American history. When the main party arrived, Sacagawea suddenly recognized the chief of the Shoshones. He was her brother, who had not seen her since the day the Hidatsas carried her away in a raid several years earlier. Sacagawea "danced for the joyful sight," Clark wrote, "and those Indians sang all the way to their camp." With Sacagawea interpreting, the Shoshones agreed to sell the expedition all the horses they needed.

On foot and on horseback, the Corps of Discovery headed across what one of them called "the most terrible mountains I ever beheld." Snows began falling. Fallen trees and rocks blocked their path. Horses tumbled down slopes that one explorer said were steeper than the roof of a house. "I have been wet and as cold in every part [of my body] as I ever was in my life," Clark wrote in his journal in mid-September. Still more mountains stretched before them. Desperate with hunger, they shot and ate a coyote and a raven, killed and ate two of their horses, and even chewed on their candles.

At last they stumbled down from the mountains, almost more dead than alive. There, on the Clearwater River, the Nez Percés found them. They, too, had never seen a white man, but they gave the starving strangers dried salmon and the roots of plants to eat. The Indians assured Lewis and Clark that it was now possible to reach the sea by water, and they permitted the expedition to fell five trees for canoes. They also promised always to remain at peace with the United States. Lewis wrote that he would never forget the generosity of the Nez Percés: "I think we can justly affirm, to the honor of this people, that they are the most hospitable, honest, and sincere people that we have met on our voyage."

Lewis and Clark moved quickly now, down the Clearwater River, then the Snake, riding with currents, one explorer remembered, "swifter than any horse could run." By late October, they were on the broad Columbia and seeing signs that they were drawing near the Pacific coast, where European vessels had been landing for decades. In the Indian villages they visited, brass teakettles hung over campfires. Some Indians wore the blue jackets and round hats traded by sailors. A few spoke small snatches of English —*musket, knife, file,* and other words.

Went up and down rocky mountains all day. Some men threaten to kill a colt to eat, they being hungry.

— Sergeant John Ordway, Lewis and Clark expedition

In early November, the river widened even farther, and they could detect the rise and fall of tidal movement in the water. On a rainy morning, they pushed on until Clark saw the fog lifting. "Ocean in view!" he hurriedly wrote in his journal. "O! the joy."

For four centuries, Europeans from different nations had been entering the West from different directions, pursuing different myths. Without the help from the native peoples who had lived on those lands for thousands of years, none would have survived for long. Yet each intruder had laid claim to the region, as if he were the first to discover it, as if the people already living on it did not exist.

Now it was the Americans' turn. The Corps of Discovery had come, Clark estimated, 4,162 miles from St. Louis. They had failed to find the Northwest Passage (because there wasn't one to find). But they had traced the Missouri and the Columbia Rivers and crossed the Rocky Mountains to the sea, as President Jefferson had wished, and they had placed their young country in the international race to claim and control the West.

At a point overlooking the surf, Clark took his knife and carved a message in the bark of a tree: "William Clark, December 3rd, 1805. By Land. From the U States."

Empire Upon the Trails
1806–1848

When Lewis and Clark finally returned to St. Louis in September of 1806, they brought back eyewitness accounts of the western territory that Thomas Jefferson had purchased from France. For the first time, Americans began to understand the rich variety of wildlife and land beyond the Mississippi River. Some began to dream of going there themselves.

But other people and other nations claimed parts of the West, too. The new Republic of Mexico—once a colony of Spain—controlled Texas, the Southwest, and California. England claimed the Pacific Northwest. Russia had Alaska and was looking to expand south. And a host of Indian peoples, who had called the West home for centuries, held fast to their lands.

Still, in the wake of Lewis and Clark, Americans began moving west between 1806 and 1848. They came for many different reasons—for adventure, for riches, for God, for escape, and most of all for land. At first they came in small numbers, willing to adjust and make their way in other people's worlds. But regardless of their individual reasons for *going* west, once they arrived, the Americans soon decided to make the West—all of it—their own.

•◆• •◆• •◆•

Joseph Lafayette Meek was from Washington County, Virginia, one of fifteen children born to a prosperous planter. When his mother died and his father remarried a strict and domineering woman, Meek ran off to the West. He was only nineteen, but he quickly became known as a "mountain man."

The mountain men were fur trappers. Their job was to catch beavers and other animals and send their pelts and skins back east, where they were used for gentlemen's hats and ladies' coats. Fur companies representing England, Russia, Mexico, and the United States all competed for the western fur trade, and the mountain men they hired came from every part of the globe. There were black trappers as well as white; men from Europe and Central America; even native Hawaiians, recruited from their small Pacific islands to toil in the western vastness. French trappers outnumbered Americans four to one. In Oregon, Iroquois and Delaware Indians from the East made up a third of the mountain men.

Joe Meek

Meek spent eleven years in the mountains. Like the other trappers, he made friends with some Indian tribes and enemies of others. He married a Nez Percé woman but also narrowly escaped death at the hands of the Blackfeet and Bannock. He traveled relentlessly, always searching for beaver streams that had not yet been overtrapped—across the deserts to California, up and down the Rockies from New Mexico to Canada, and one time into a strange landscape he said was "smoking with the vapor

A mountain man's life was filled with danger.

from boiling springs and burning with gasses issuing from small craters." Few people believed his (and other mountain men's) descriptions of the place, which would one day become Yellowstone National Park.

Trapping was a hard life. Once, Meek was nearly killed by a grizzly bear. Another time, on a dare, he touched a grizzly with his bare hand. The constant work in ice-cold rivers ruined many men's health. Sometimes, Meek remembered, there was nothing to eat: "I have held my hands in an ant hill until they were covered with ants, then greedily licked them off. I have taken the soles of my moccasins, crisped them in the fire, and eaten them. We used to take a kettle of hot water, catch the crickets and throw them in, and when they stopped kicking, eat them."

I have held my hands in an ant hill until they were covered with ants, then greedily licked them off.

—Joe Meek

Each summer, their reward came when the mountain men and their Indian allies gathered in one place to hold what was called a rendezvous. Caravans from St. Louis arrived to collect furs in exchange for supplies

After the yearly rendezvous,
a supply train heads back
to St. Louis.

for the next year. Once the business was conducted, the rendezvous turned into a wild celebration—a "crazy drunk," Meek said—and by the time it was over, most of the trappers headed back into the mountains, having spent their year's earnings on whiskey, gambling, and tobacco. Few of them ever got rich from their rough and dangerous life.

The trappers had been the first Americans to go west in any numbers, but in the late 1830s their era suddenly came to an end. Styles changed in the big cities of the East and Europe. People now wanted silk rather than beaver for fashionable clothes.

The mountain men were out of work. Some returned east. Others used their knowledge of the West to become scouts and guides for wagon trains and explorers.

Joe Meek had had enough of the mountains and wanted to settle down. But instead of returning to Virginia, he took his Nez Percé wife and children *all* the way west, to a spot near a British trading post in the disputed land of Oregon. There, Meek joined a few other Americans who were already talking about making the Pacific Coast part of the United States.

"I want to live long enough to see Oregon securely American," he said, "so I can say I was born in Washington County, United States, and died in Washington County, United States."

More Americans were beginning to come west now, following the mountain men's footsteps but pursuing entirely different dreams.

Missionaries from the East believed it was their religious duty to convert western Indians. In the late 1830s, Marcus and Narcissa Whitman took the long Overland Trail to what was called Oregon Country (what is now Oregon, Washington, and Idaho) to preach to the Cayuse. With them went Henry and Eliza Spalding, who set up a mission among the Nez Percés, the Indians who had befriended Lewis and Clark. Most of the missionaries failed to persuade the Native Americans to abandon their old beliefs for Christianity, but the preacher's letters back home convinced many easterners that land in the West was both fertile and free for the taking.

At the same time, thousands of American settlers were welcomed into the northern Mexican province of Tejas (which would later be known as Texas), as long as they became Catholics and swore allegiance to Mexico. A handful of American merchants moved into the province of New Mexico and opened a profitable trading business between Missouri and Santa Fe. And New England businessmen showed up by ship in California, where

A Mormon wagon train
on its way to Utah

they married the daughters of prominent Mexican families and became rich exchanging goods manufactured in the East for western cattle hides and beef tallow.

Not everyone came west by choice. Followers of a new religion called the Church of Jesus Christ of Latter-day Saints, or Mormons, found themselves persecuted in Missouri and Illinois. When their leader, Joseph Smith, was murdered by a mob, they decided, with the help of a new leader, Brigham Young, to leave the boundaries of the United States and start over where they might be left alone. The deserts and mountains around the Great Salt Lake, in what is now Utah, seemed like the perfect place, so they began an exodus to their new Promised Land.

And in the 1830s, Congress created a huge new "Indian Territory," stretching from Texas to the middle Missouri River, meant to be a place the Indians would have to themselves forever. One by one, under a plan called removal, Indian peoples from the East were forced to give up their homelands and move west—the Delaware, Ottawa, Shawnee, and Potawatomi; the Sac and Fox, Miami and Kickapoo; the Choctaws, Chickasaws, Creeks, and Seminoles. In all, ninety thousand Indians were relocated. Some went willingly, but most did not. The Cherokees were driven from their homes at bayonet point; two thousand of them died on what the Cherokees remember as the Trail of Tears.

A pioneer family

But by the mid-1840s, the most common group heading west was farming families, seeking new lands to settle. Just across the Missouri River was good farmland, but it was Indian Territory and off limits to white settlement. Nearly two thousand miles away were Oregon and California. One was claimed by both England and the United States; the

COVERED WAGON DAYS IN WYOMING MEYERS COPY.

A wagon train crosses the sagebrush hills of Wyoming.

other was still part of Mexico. Despite the distance and uncertain national ownership, however, constant reports of good soil and a gentle, healthy climate began luring more and more pioneers to make the long trek. At first they numbered in the hundreds. But soon they went by the thousands—so many that their wagon wheels etched a trail in soil and stone that would mark their paths for generations to remember.

In the spring of 1844, a crowded wagon lumbered westward over the prairie. In it rode the Sager family—Henry and Naomi and their six children, two boys and four girls, ages three to thirteen. They had already moved four times in the last four years, always a little farther west in search of land that was more fertile and less expensive. Now, as one of the children remembered, their father "got the Oregon fever," and they were headed across the continent as part of a wagon train.

Heavy rains were falling, so the Sager children were confined to their covered wagon for mile after lurching mile. They grew seasick from the motion. One evening, when they huddled too close to a campfire, their bedclothes caught on fire. As they crossed Indian Territory, nervous guards fired into the darkness at the slightest sound. No Indians ever attacked, but one night two girls out for a stroll were nearly hit by the guards' bullets.

In late May, Mrs. Sager gave birth to her seventh child—a baby girl named Henrietta—in a damp

In the month of April 1844, my father got the Oregon fever and we started west.
— *Matilda Sager*

tent near a flooded river. Farther on, the skies finally cleared, and on July 4 the wagon train rested to celebrate the holiday. A young couple got married, and people played music that to nine-year-old Catherine Sager "sounded out clear and sweet on the evening air, while gay talk and merry laughter went on around the campfire."

So far, the trip had been an adventure for the Sager children, despite the discomforts. There was always something new along the trail. Buffalo herds thundered by, and the men raced off to hunt them. As the wagons followed the Platte River into what is now western Nebraska, strange landmarks appeared on the horizon—Courthouse Rock, Chimney Rock, and Scotts Bluff, exciting signs that they would soon leave the prairies behind. Catherine, the oldest of the girls, had learned to jump from the front seat of the moving wagon whenever she wanted to walk out and explore on her own. But on July 30, as they neared what is now Wyoming, her long dress caught on the wagon when she tried to leap down. She was tossed to the ground. Before her father could stop the oxen, both wagon wheels rolled over one of her legs. "My dear child," he said when he reached his daughter, "your leg is broken all to pieces!" For the remainder of the trip, Catherine either rode in the jolting wagon or walked with crutches. But the worst was still ahead.

Catherine Sager in later years

As they entered the mountains, a sickness called "camp fever" struck the caravan. Two women died, then a little girl. Three of the Sager children came down with burning fevers and nausea, and finally Mr. Sager did, too. Unlike his children, he never recovered. "The evening before he died, we crossed the Green River and camped on its bank," Catherine recalled. "Looking upon me as I lay helplessly by his side, he said, 'Poor child! What will become of you?' Father expired the next morning, and was buried on the bank of the Green River, his coffin…hastily dug out of the trunk of a tree."

Fatherless, the Sagers pushed on. Mrs. Sager hired a young man to drive their wagon, but after a few days, he disappeared with Henry's gun to join his girlfriend in the wagon train ahead of them.

At last they crossed the border into Oregon Country, but on the dusty trail along the Snake River, Naomi Sager became delirious with fever. She talked as if her husband were still alive and cried out in pain with every bump of the wagon. Her children tried desperately to help her, but it was no use. "We traveled over a very rough road, and she moaned pitifully all day," according to Catherine. "When we camped for the night, her pulse was nearly gone.…She lived but a few moments more, and her last words were, 'Oh Henry, if you only knew how we have suffered!'"

Matilda Sager

Pioneers resting on the long trail

The children buried their mother, wrapped in a bedsheet, in a shallow grave along the trail, with willow brush and a wooden board to mark the spot. It was now late September, and the first snows were falling

The teams were then hitched to the wagon and the train drove on... and we were orphans, the oldest fourteen years old and the youngest five months old.

— Catherine Sager

in the mountains. The wagon train had to hurry on, and the seven Sager children—now orphans—had to move along with it.

At last they reached Cayuse country, where Marcus and Narcissa Whitman had established a mission. The Whitmans' two-year-old daughter had drowned several years earlier, and in her grief Narcissa had been taking in other children, including a half-Indian daughter of Joe Meek. A messenger rode ahead to inform the missionaries about the Sager children's plight.

A few days later, after six grueling months, two thousand miles, and the loss of both their parents, the Sagers finally reached the end of their trail. Narcissa Whitman had already agreed to adopt them and came out to meet them. "She had on a dark calico dress and gingham sunbonnet," Catherine recalled, "and we thought as we shyly looked at her that she was the prettiest woman we had ever seen."

Henrietta Naomi Sager, who was born during the trip to Oregon

For the people already living in the West—Indians and the Mexican descendants of Spanish colonists—the arrival of American newcomers from the East at first seemed like good news.

Tribes that traded with the fur companies received manufactured goods and guns that made them richer and sometimes more powerful than their enemies. Missionaries like the Whitmans and Spaldings initially appeared to offer some of the white man's "power," which the Indians hoped merely to add to their own beliefs. The wagon trains of pioneers often needed food and supplies that the tribes sold along the trails.

But the newcomers brought trouble, too. Diseases such as smallpox and cholera spread from the whites to the Indians, who had no immunities against them. Some tribes lost more than half of their people to these

29

invisible but deadly enemies. Others began to worry about the increasing number of white people streaming west. "We have plenty of buffalo, beaver, deer, and other wild animals," a Pawnee chief named Petalesharo told President James Monroe during a visit to Washington. "We have everything we want. We have plenty of land—if you will keep your people off of it."

In the newly formed Indian Territory, relocated tribes from the East sometimes fought with native tribes over hunting grounds. The Comanches and Kiowas drove some Indians originally from Georgia off of the southern buffalo plains. Farther north, the Cheyenne and Arapahos lost a hundred warriors against the better-armed Potawatomis, who lost just four. The U.S. army finally had to enforce a tense peace.

We have everything we want. We have plenty of land—if you will keep your people off of it.

— Petalesharo, Pawnee chief

And some tribes who had welcomed missionaries soon regretted it. The Cayuse in particular began to resent the Whitmans, who refused to pay for their mission land, demanded that the Cayuse give up all their traditional sacred beliefs, and seemed more interested in helping white pioneers than the Indians they had come west to "save." Three years after the Sagers arrived, a wagon train stopping at the mission brought measles with it. Half of the Cayuse died, including most of their children. Blaming the missionaries for all their misfortunes, the Cayuse murdered Marcus and Narcissa Whitman, burned down the mission buildings, killed eleven other whites, and took many more hostage. Three of the Sager children and Joe Meek's daughter were among those who died in the uprising.

The four surviving Sager girls were eventually freed, and five Cayuse warriors gave themselves up so that the rest of the tribe would not be hunted down. The warriors were sentenced to death, with Joe Meek acting as the hangman. Before he went to the gallows, one of the Cayuse was asked why he had surrendered. "Did not your missionaries teach us that Christ died to save his people?" he answered. "So we die to save *our* people."

The Hispanic people in Mexico's northern provinces also experienced a shift in their relations with the Americans. In California and New Mexico, the leading families at first prospered from American business but soon became concerned that they would be outnumbered and overwhelmed. In Texas, the Spanish-speaking Tejanos joined forces with American settlers to rebel against the Mexican dictator Antonio López de Santa Anna, only to feel that their part in the revolution was forgotten.

One of the rebels was young Juan Seguin, whose father had warmly greeted Stephen Austin, the first American colonist to Texas, in 1821. In 1835, when Seguin was still in his twenties, he recruited some fellow Tejano ranchers to drive a Mexican force from San Antonio. And the next year, he was among the men devoted to Texas's freedom who were surrounded by Santa Anna's army in the Alamo. "I would joyfully perish on the field of battle shouting the war cry, 'God and Liberty, Victory or Death!'" he said.

Juan Seguin

At great risk to his life, Seguin smuggled a plea for help from William Travis, the Alamo commander, through enemy lines. But the help did not come, and Seguin was on his way back to his comrades on March 6, 1836, when Santa Anna's men destroyed the Alamo and killed its defenders. Six weeks later, Seguin led a company of Tejanos as part of Sam Houston's Texas army, which defeated Santa Anna at the Battle of San Jacinto.

The Alamo

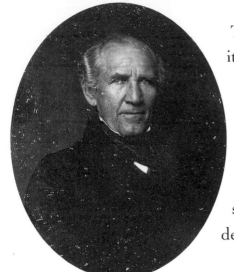

Sam Houston

Texas declared itself an independent republic, with Houston as its president. Seguin was made a senator and twice was elected mayor of San Antonio, where he presided over a burial ceremony for his friends who had died defending the Alamo. But the new republic was soon overrun by Americans who distrusted the native Tejanos. Rumors were started that Seguin's loyalty was with Mexico, not Texas. Finally he was forced to slip south across the border, fleeing the land whose independence he had helped win.

By the mid-1840s, some Americans were demanding that the Republic of Texas, the Mexican provinces of New Mexico and California, and the British possessions in Oregon be added to the United States. Expanding all the way to the Pacific, they said, was the country's "manifest destiny," a preordained plan that nothing should, or could, prevent.

"The American realizes that Progress is God," wrote William Gilpin, one of the biggest boosters of expansion. "He clearly recognizes and accepts the continental mission of his country and his people.... The pioneer army perpetually advances [and] strikes to the front. Empire plants itself upon the trails."

Not everyone shared Gilpin's view. "What do we want with this region of savages and wild beasts, of deserts, of shifting sands and whirlwinds of dust, of cactus and prairie dogs?" asked Senator Daniel Webster of Massachusetts. And in Mexico, a government official named José Maria Tornel y Mendivil warned

[It is] our manifest destiny to overspread the continent.

—*John L. O'Sullivan,* UNITED STATES MAGAZINE AND DEMOCRATIC REVIEW, 1845

that for years the Americans' "roving spirit" had created a "frenzy to gain control of that which rightfully belongs to its neighbors."

Then, in 1844, Americans narrowly elected a new president, James K. Polk, who promised to extend the nation's boundaries.

First, Texas willingly joined the Union as the twenty-eighth state. Next, Polk threatened hostilities with England over the Pacific Northwest, until the British abandoned their claims to what would one day be Idaho,

Washington, and Oregon. Finally, when Mexico refused to sell the Southwest and California in 1846, President Polk convinced Congress to declare war and sent armies south to fight it—a bloody, desperate struggle that lasted more than a year and a half, cost thousands of lives, and ended only when American troops finally stormed into Mexico City.

The loss of Texas will inevitably result in the loss of New Mexico and the Californias. Little by little our territory will be absorbed.

—*José María Tornel y Mendívil, Mexican official*

On July 4, 1848, thousands of people in Washington, D.C., turned out to see President Polk lay the cornerstone of a new monument—a giant stone tower to honor George Washington, the nation's first president.

President Washington's United States had ended at the Mississippi. But now Polk was the president of a *continental* nation, which stretched from sea to sea and encompassed the West. In only one generation—by bluff and intimidation, by sacrifice and outright conquest—Americans had seized it all.

Standing next to the president at the ceremony was Joe Meek, whose fondest wish had come true. Born in Washington County, Virginia, the old mountain man was now sheriff of a brand-new Washington County—in Oregon Territory.

President James K. Polk

The Speck of the Future
1848-1855

*James Marshall at
Sutter's mill*

By 1848, the United States claimed virtually all of the West. The Louisiana Purchase, the annexation of Texas and Oregon, and the war with Mexico had stretched the nation's boundaries all the way to the Pacific.

Still, much of the West was American in name only. So far, fewer than fifteen thousand Americans had made the long overland journey across the continent. To most people living east of the Mississippi River, the West seemed distant, dangerous, and totally unknown—hardly part of the United States at all, and certainly not worth the risk to go and see for themselves.

Then, on the American River in California, something was discovered that would change everything—for California, for the West, and for the country.

•◆• •◆• •◆•

James Marshall, a carpenter from New Jersey, had come west in 1844, traveling to Oregon in the same wagon train that brought the Sager family. By 1848 he had drifted down the coast to California and was working for John Sutter, a Swiss-born rancher who had carved out a small empire for himself in central California—a fort and fifty thousand acres of land, fields, and orchards tended by Indian laborers.

On the morning of January 24, 1848, Marshall walked out to inspect a sawmill he and his crew were building for Sutter on a bend of the south fork of the American River. In a ditch the men had been digging along the streambed, Marshall noticed something glittering on the bottom. He reached down and picked it up. "Hey, boys," he called out to the others as he turned a yellow piece of rock in his hand, "by God, I believe I've found a gold mine."

Marshall wrapped his discovery in a handkerchief and took it to Sutter's Fort, where the two men followed the instructions in an old encyclopedia to test the nugget's mineral content. It was nearly pure gold.

At first, they were able to keep their astounding news somewhat secret. The mill workers did a little prospecting after hours, and Sutter informed his neighbor, Mariano Guadalupe Vallejo, the biggest landowner in California, that there would be riches enough for them both. But word soon spread, and a few curious gold seekers followed the rumors back to Sutter's mill.

One of them was Sam Brannan, a Mormon who quickly realized that his stores—stocked with picks,

Sam Brannan

35
•◆•

pans, shovels, and other supplies—would be gold mines themselves, if only more people found out about the gold strike. So Brannan returned to San Francisco and made sure that *everyone* found out. On May 12, he walked through the small town's streets, waving a bottle full of gold dust and shouting, "Gold! Gold! Gold from the American River!"

Within a few weeks, three out of every four men in San Francisco had left town to dig for gold. "The blacksmith dropped his hammer, the farmer his sickle, the baker his loaf," an official in nearby Monterey wrote. "All were off for the mines, some on horses, some on carts, and some on crutches.... I have only a community of women left, and a gang of prisoners, with here and there a soldier who will give his captain the slip at the first chance. I don't blame the fellow a whit; [why settle for] seven dollars a month, when others [digging gold] are making two or three hundred a day!"

The gold rush had begun.

During the summer of 1848, gold seemed to be everywhere in the streams and rivers of the Sierra Nevada foothills. Some prospectors brought in crude machinery and hired Indians to do the work. In one case, fifty Indians dug out 273 pounds of gold in just two months for their employer. Other miners got their gold using nothing but jackknives and spoons to pry it from rocks or scoop it from sandbars. "My average income is about 150 dollars a day," one Californian wrote home to Missouri. "My little girls can make from five to twenty-five dollars per day washing gold in pans."

A frenzy seized my soul. Piles of gold rose up before me. In short, I had a very violent attack of the gold fever.

— Hubert Howe Bancroft

As news of the bonanza fanned out from California—most often by ship—it touched off a frenzy in every place it reached. Two thirds of the American men in Oregon raced south in search of gold. Hawaiians and then Chinese sailed across the Pacific. From Mexico, where the Spanish had been mining gold for three centuries, so many men headed north, one person reported, that it seemed as if an "entire state" was on the move. Thousands more set off from every port in South America.

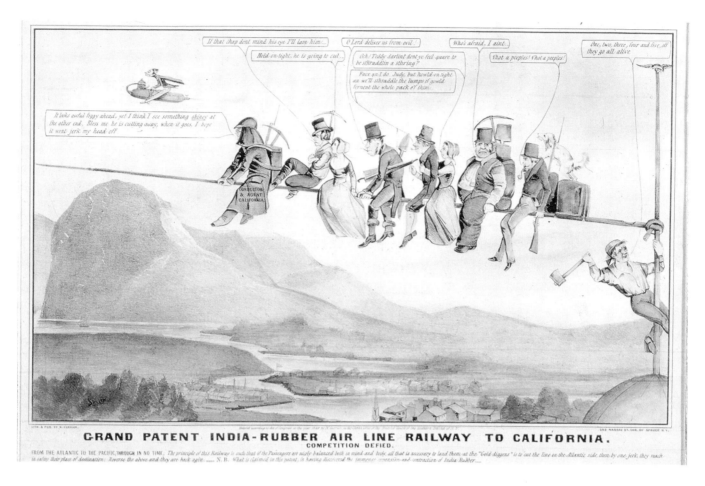

By early December, an official report on the gold discovery had reached President Polk, who used it in his annual message to Congress. The report said that four thousand prospectors in California were gleaning up to fifty thousand dollars worth of gold a day and that Sam Brannan's stores were clearing two thousand dollars a day in profits supplying them. But what really caught Americans' attention was a tea box filled with gold dust, which the President placed on display for everyone to see—proof that the fabulous tales were true.

Now even more people became convinced that a fast and easy fortune waited for them in California. And they would get it, they decided, in 1849.

They called themselves forty-niners, and that year they created one of the most remarkable human stampedes in history—nearly ninety thousand people, mostly men, swarming to California from every corner of the

A forty-niner proudly displays picks and shovels on his shirt.

globe. The only thing they had in common was that they planned to get rich quick and return home in glory.

William Swain was a farmer from Youngstown, New York, well educated and living a comfortable life with his young wife and new baby. But the tales of California gold proved impossible for him to resist. By April of 1849, Swain was already in Missouri—along with thirty-five thousand other Americans—waiting for the spring rains to end so his wagon train could start across the prairies on the overland route to California. "I am coming back," he confidently wrote his wife, "with a pocket full of rocks!"

Vicente Pérez Rosales came from a rich family in Chile that had fallen on hard times. Rosales had tried everything he could think of to restore his family's fortune—ranching, distilling whiskey, making barrels, even smuggling. Nothing had worked. Now he and his three younger brothers were sailing from Valparaiso to stake everything on California's gold.

Whichever route the forty-niners took, they faced hardships and dangers. On the Overland Trail, cholera killed more than fifteen hundred gold seekers that summer. Swain got sick, but recovered, only to endure more troubles. Hailstorms knocked men to the ground. Scorching deserts killed oxen. Early snows in the mountain passes made streams so icy, Swain said, that when he forded them, "I thought my flesh would drop from my bones." The trek took him seven months and was "the hardest job I ever had."

In 1849, San Francisco's harbor was jammed with ships.

The sea route was quicker but more expensive. And the vessels were sometimes unsafe—one man survived three shipwrecks on his way to San Francisco—and always overcrowded and unsanitary. "Seasickness is widespread," Rosales wrote during his voyage. "The sides of the ships are covered with dripping vomit, and the cabin and the ladders as well. Everywhere you see green faces and hear the sounds of men wretching."

We are a mixed lot — Frenchmen, Englishmen, Germans, Italians, Chileans, nabobs and beggars, . . . a Chinaman, a Hindu, a Russian, and a native Californio, all trying to converse. — Vicente Pérez Rosales

Once they finally arrived, the forty-niners shared something else in common: They were all stunned that so many others had made the same decision they had made. The gold region's riverbanks now teemed with thousands upon thousands of prospectors. "We are a mixed lot," Rosales reported, "Frenchmen, Englishmen, Germans, Italians, Chileans, nabobs and beggars, . . . a Chinaman, a Hindu, a Russian, and a native Californio" —all chasing the same dream.

·◆·

Miners at work in the goldfields

By 1849, the easy pickings were over. With the easily found surface gold already taken, the new arrivals spent most of the day moving rocks in riverbeds, digging deeper and deeper. It was hard and monotonous—more like "canal digging, ditching, laying stone walls, plowing and hoeing potatoes," one miner wrote, than a treasure hunt. Swain called it "a dog's life."

And it was usually unrewarding. What little gold the forty-niners sifted from the mounds of dirt and rock went to pay for food and supplies, which were far more expensive in the mining camps than back home. Swain complained that a pound of dried apples, which would have cost four cents in New York, sold for two dollars in California. Eggs were fifty cents each. A jar of pickles went for eight dollars. He paid two dollars to have his mail brought from San Francisco, where the nearest post office was.

The men who made the fortunes were gentlemen who lacked the hardihood to go prospecting for gold.

— *Vicente Pérez Rosales*

"The men who made the fortunes," Vicente Pérez Rosales noted, "were gentlemen who lacked the hardihood to go prospecting for gold." California's mines produced more than half a billion dollars' worth of new wealth in less than ten years. But most of it ended up in the pockets of merchants, bankers, lawyers, cooks, and saloon keepers—anyone who filled the miners' needs.

Levi Strauss, a German immigrant who had done poorly selling needles and ribbons and pins door-to-door in New York, turned up in San Francisco with some cotton material he thought would be perfect for making tents. It turned out to be wrong for tents, but Strauss used it to make a miner a pair of durable pants. Soon other miners were asking for "those pants of Levi's."

A Chinese man named Wah Lee opened San Francisco's first large hand laundry in 1851. Wealthy San Franciscans had been sending their good shirts more than two thousand miles to Hawaii and Hong Kong to have them washed and ironed, at rates that ran as high as twelve dollars a dozen. Wah Lee charged just five dollars—and made a killing.

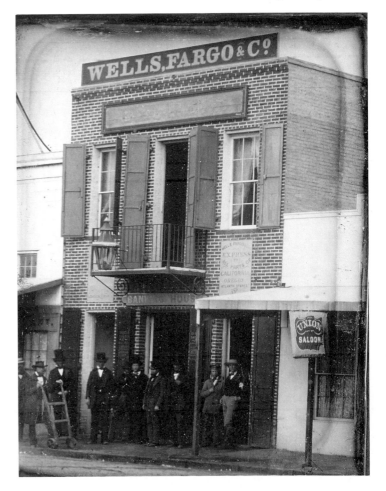

Wells, Fargo opened offices throughout California.

When the American Express company refused to open offices in California because it seemed so far away from the firm's headquarters in the East, two of its partners, Henry Wells and William Fargo, started their own business serving the miners. In time, their company was exchanging cash for gold dust, shipping money east, even operating a private mail service that was more reliable than the post office. Wells made only one brief trip to California, and Fargo never came west at all. But Wells, Fargo and Company became the West's wealthiest business, with offices in nearly every western town.

When she and her husband arrived in California, Luzena Stanley Wilson set up a table under the trees, bought provisions at a nearby store, and served twenty hungry miners a meal for a dollar each. Soon she was feeding two hundred men, at twenty-five dollars per week. She built an inn, hired a cook and waiters, even became a banker for the men she fed—and earned far more than her husband ever did panning for gold. "Many a night have I shut my oven door on two milk cans filled high with bags of gold dust," Wilson wrote, "and I must have had more than two hundred thousand dollars lying unprotected in my bedroom."

The gold rush turned San Francisco into the West's biggest and richest city.

California was transformed overnight by the gold rush. In just three years, its non-Indian population skyrocketed from fourteen thousand to nearly 250,000 people.

Before the gold discovery at Sutter's mill, San Francisco had a population of nine hundred. Three years later, thirty-five thousand people lived there. And what had once been a small village was now the West's first full-fledged city—with a dozen daily newspapers, fifteen fire companies, three hospitals, eighteen churches, and 537 saloons. House lots that once sold for $16.50 now commanded prices of forty-five thousand dollars. Fires repeatedly broke out, many of them started deliberately by looters, and ravaged the young city. But each time, San Francisco rebuilt—and kept growing.

The American arrivals demanded immediate statehood for California, and they got it in 1850. And in the overcrowded mining camps, they began insisting that there was no room for anyone but themselves.

They pressured the new California legislature to pass a monthly tax of twenty dollars on all miners who were not United States citizens. Many of the Mexican miners left the goldfields, unable to pay the tax. When a group of French miners dared display their flag, they, too, were driven from their claims. But the Chinese paid the fee and refused to leave. There were more than twenty thousand Chinese in California by this time, and the "foreign miners' tax" they paid constituted half of the state government's revenues. Some Americans resorted to intimidation to get rid of unwanted miners. They burned down the Chinese miners' shacks and beat, flogged, and even murdered them.

The ill will of the Yankee rabble against sons of other nations was rising. — Vicente Pérez Rosales

"The ill will of the Yankee rabble against sons of other nations was rising," wrote Rosales, who hung on in the goldfields despite taxes and

A Chinese graveyard
in California

threats. "This mutual bad feeling explains the bloody hostilities and atrocities we witnessed every day in this land of gold and hope."

Native Californios also were discriminated against, even though their families had settled in the area nearly a hundred years before the Americans' arrival. Mariano Guadalupe Vallejo had welcomed the Americans at first. He helped write the new state's constitution and served in its first state senate. Then his sprawling estate in the Sonoma Valley was invaded by squatters, and lawsuits over his land claims ate away his fortune. Eventually, Vallejo's 250,000 acres were reduced to fewer than three hundred acres, and like other Californios, he was considered an alien in the land of his birth.

Mariano Guadalupe Vallejo

But the incredible influx of outsiders was hardest of all on California's Indians. At first, some worked in the goldfields, until they, along with other so-called foreigners, were forced out. All the mining activity ruined their hunting and fishing grounds, and new diseases swept through their villages. One California law allowed Indians, in effect, to be forced against their will into working for whites, while another law prohibited them from testifying in court against whites. Some mining towns even offered bounties of five dollars for every Native American scalp or head brought in to city hall.

"The miners are sometimes guilty of the most brutal acts with the Indians, such as killing the squaws and papooses," William Swain wrote. "Such incidents have fallen under my notice that would make humanity weep and men disown their race."

There were some 150,000 Indians in California before the forty-niners came. By 1870, there would be fewer than thirty thousand. It was the worst slaughter of Indian peoples in United States history.

•◆•

In the early days of the gold rush, Indians worked alongside white miners. But when gold grew scarce, whites drove them from the goldfields.

The gold rush transformed not just California but the entire West.

Indian tribes along the crowded overland trails suffered from the cholera spread by the forty-niners, and others found it hard to find buffalo where the wagon trains' oxen had eaten the prairie grasses. "Since the white man has made a road across our land and killed our game, we are hungry and there is nothing for us to eat," the Shoshone chief Washakie told a federal agent. "Our women and children cry for food, and we have no food to give them."

Meanwhile, politicians on both coasts began talking seriously of

Such a thing as a white man being punished for outraging an Indian was unheard of.

— General George Crook

building a railroad all the way across the continent to connect the East with the sudden wealth and American population in California. The West was becoming part of the nation now as never before.

And as thousands of discouraged forty-niners began heading home, many of them paused to pan for gold in places they had bypassed in their hurry to California. New discoveries of what was called "the speck of the future" were made in Idaho, Oregon, New Mexico, and Arizona, in

With each new gold discovery, more towns sprang up across the West.

Montana's Last Chance Gulch, Pikes Peak in Colorado, and in Nevada, the great Comstock Lode.

Wherever gold and silver were found, the pattern set in California repeated itself. Americans rushed in. Towns sprang up. New, unimagined wealth was created. And Indian peoples—the Apaches and Paiutes, the Shoshones and Coeur D'Alenes, the Cheyenne and Nez Percés, and many more—found themselves outnumbered in their own lands.

James Marshall, who had started it all in 1848, lived to regret his discovery. Miners followed him wherever he went, convinced that Marshall was blessed with uncanny powers at finding gold. When he failed to find more, they grew angry and even threatened to hang him. Another time, a mob went after him because he defended the rights of local Indians. He died, penniless, in a cabin overlooking the American River, where he had once dreamed of becoming a rich man.

John Sutter, too, was ruined by the gold rush he had helped start. Squatters overran his vast estate, ruined his wheat fields, and stole and killed his cattle. Finally someone burned his house down. Sutter went broke, started drinking heavily, and eventually moved out of the West completely.

Sam Brannan claimed to be California's first millionaire. With the profits from his stores, he bought a fifth of the land in San Francisco and a quarter of Sacramento. But he quickly lost his fortune in other schemes and died just as poor as Sutter and Marshall.

Vicente Pérez Rosales and his three brothers stubbornly stayed on in California, despite the hostility of the Americans, until one of San Francisco's fires finally burned them out. "Two and a half months later," he wrote, "we were [back] in peaceful Chile, tenderly embracing our mother, poor as ever, but satisfied that we had not abandoned the fort before the last shot was fired." In his later years, he became a member of Chile's national senate.

William Swain also never found the easy fortune he had sought. By the fall of 1850, he was weak with fever, sick of being separated from his family, and no richer than the day he had left his wife and baby for California a year and a half earlier. "My expectations are not realized," he wrote to his wife. "We have been unlucky—or rather, being inexperienced, we selected a poor spot for a location and staked all on it, and it has proved worth nothing. . . . I have got enough of California and am coming home as fast as I can."

Back in upstate New York, he began farming again as if he'd never been away and became the most successful peach grower in Niagara County. He and his wife, Sabrina, had three more children, who grew up listening to their father's stories of the days he had crossed the entire continent to search for gold.

Although most forty-niners—like Swain and Rosales—returned home with nothing more than adventures to tell their families, for some, California did turn out to be a land of dreams. Nancy Gooch was brought west as a slave in 1849 but was emancipated when California entered the Union as a free state in 1850. She took jobs as a cook and washerwoman in the town of Coloma and managed to save seven hundred dollars— enough to buy the freedom of her son and his wife back in Missouri.

They came to California, raised a family, and worked hard planting orchards and vineyards. Eventually they bought the site of Sutter's sawmill on the south fork of the American River, where the gold rush had begun.

Death Runs Riot
1855-1868

In the years following the California gold rush, Americans moved west in ever larger numbers, searching for new treasure, clearing land, building towns and cities—starting over.

But these new settlers also brought with them the nation's oldest, most divisive issue: slavery. The West, seen as the land of hope and new beginnings, soon became a breeding ground for the hatred and bloodshed that would eventually engulf the whole country and threaten the survival of the nation itself.

In the East, the Civil War was fought by great armies. But in the West, the battle lines were less clear—and more personal. Most of the killing was done by ordinary citizens. Neighbor slaughtered neighbor, families fought families, and random violence consumed whole communities. Indians, too, were drawn into the struggle and made to pay a terrible price.

And when the Civil War finally ended, the soldiers who had helped free the slaves in the East would be sent to conquer the Indians of the West.

•◆• •◆• •◆•

In the spring of 1855, the Reverend Charles Lovejoy of Croydon, New Hampshire, and his wife, Julia Louisa, crossed the Missouri River with their children into the newly created Kansas Territory.

Thousands of settlers were pouring in that year to stake claims in what had recently been Indian lands. But the Lovejoys—and others like them—were a different kind of American pioneer, not interested in gold, land, or adventure.

They were abolitionists, Americans opposed to slavery. And they had come west determined to keep slavery out of Kansas. "A great work is to be done," Julia wrote home to a New Hampshire newspaper. "Kansas is the great battlefield where a mighty conflict is to be waged with the monster slavery, and he will be routed and slain. Amen and Amen."

For fifty years, the United States had been expanding westward. And each time that North and South argued over whether new territories should be slave or free, Congress had worked out a compromise that kept the country together. Now, the Kansas and Nebraska Act proposed that the settlers, not Congress, decide whether to permit slavery, so

Julia Louisa Lovejoy

supporters of both sides of the old argument were encouraging people to move to Kansas for the upcoming election.

On voting day, nearly five thou-

Come on then, Gentlemen of the Slave States.... We will engage in competition for the virgin soil of Kansas. —Senator William H. Seward, New York

sand armed slavery supporters—"border ruffians," their enemies dubbed them—flooded into Kansas from Missouri. They seized voting places and cast four times as many ballots as there were voters in the territory. Then they installed a legislature that made it a crime to even criticize slavery.

Some settlers were willing to fight to keep slavery out of Kansas.

A poster announces a Free Soil meeting.

Abolitionists like the Lovejoys—called Free Soilers—held their own election, drew up a constitution outlawing slavery, and applied for admission to the Union as a free state.

Kansas now had two governments. Its people were about to go to war with one another.

Fighting erupted in the spring of 1856. After a proslavery sheriff was wounded, eight hundred border ruffians took revenge on the town of Lawrence. They destroyed two newspaper offices and burned down a hotel and the home of the Free Soil governor. Julia Lovejoy, fearing for her family's safety, fled into the woods with her one-year-old baby as the border ruffians swept by.

And on May 24, an obsessed man named John Brown called five settlers out of their cabins on Pottawatomie Creek. With the help of his sons, Brown hacked them to death with broadswords because he assumed they favored slavery. The issue, Brown believed, was a war to the death between good and evil, and "we must fight fire with fire." During the next three months, two hundred more people would die in what came to be known as "Bleeding Kansas."

We are in the midst of war — war of the most bloody kind — a war of extermination. Freedom and slavery are interlocked in deadly embrace.

—Julia Louisa Lovejoy

The Civil War was still more than four years away. But in Kansas, Julia Lovejoy wrote, "We are in the midst of war —war of the most bloody kind —a war of extermination. Freedom and slavery are interlocked in deadly embrace…and only God knoweth where it will end."

On October 16, 1859, John Brown struck again—this time in the East. Hoping to start a slave rebellion, he and a handful of other abolitionists seized the army weapons arsenal at Harper's Ferry, Virginia. Ten people were killed. Brown was captured, tried, and hanged. The whole country was now experiencing the fear that had gripped Kansas for so long.

John Brown

After Abraham Lincoln was elected president in 1860, one by one the southern slave states left the Union. And in the spring of 1861, the Civil War began.

At first, the Confederate states dreamed of extending westward to capture the rich goldfields of New Mexico, Colorado, and California. Chanting the slogan "On to San Francisco," a rebel army of 3,700 Texans moved west, winning some early victories. But in the mountains of northern New Mexico, they ran into a force of Colorado volunteers led by Major John M. Chivington. He was a big, bearlike man, a Methodist minister who sometimes preached with a revolver resting on the pulpit.

At what was called the "Gettysburg of the West," Chivington and his men stopped the Confederates at Glorieta Pass, then slipped behind their lines, climbed down a cliff, and attacked the rebel supply train. They burned eighty-five wagons and bayonetted five hundred horses and mules.

Near starvation and parched with thirst, the Texans retreated across the desert. Boots wore out. Soldiers staggered through scorching sand in bare feet and collapsed from exhaustion, dehydration, and sunstroke. Nearly fifteen hundred of them died—along with the dream of a Confederate West.

John Chivington became a Union hero.

In Indian Territory—where eastern tribes had been relocated twenty years earlier—the same issues that divided the nation tore apart the Seminoles, Chickasaws, Choctaws, Creeks, and Cherokees.

Indians enlisting in the Union army

Some in those tribes owned slaves and fought for the Confederacy; others joined the Union cause. Members of the same tribe fought one another in bloody battles and burned each others' houses to the ground. Nearly one third of the Cherokees—both soldiers and civilians—would die during the conflict. And Indian Territory would lose a higher percentage of men in the war than any state, North or South.

In western Minnesota, the Santee Sioux began to starve because Congress was preoccupied with the war and failed to vote the funds the Indians needed to buy food. They rose up, slaughtered four hundred settlers, and drove thousands more from their homes before federal troops arrived and forced them to surrender.

And in the Southwest, when federal troops had abandoned their forts to hurry east to the war, tribes such as the Apaches saw it as a chance to drive out *all* outsiders. They stole livestock, attacked settlements, and raided mining camps. General James Carleton launched a campaign to subdue them. To do it, he turned to Kit Carson, a former mountain man and explorer.

It was said that the North would be whipped. It began to be whispered that now would be a good time to go to war with the whites and get back the lands.

— Big Eagle, Santee Sioux

After forcing the Apaches to surrender, Carson was sent to bring in the Navajos. For six months, aided by Zuñi and Ute scouts, his men burned the Navajos' homes and corn crops, took their sheep, and hacked down their fruit trees. Facing starvation, more than eight thousand Navajos finally gave themselves up. In the dead of winter, they were made to march three hundred miles across New Mexico, to an arid stretch of land along the Pecos River called Bosque Redondo. There was not enough food, clothes, or supplies. Hundreds died along the way. The Navajos remember it as the Long Walk.

Kit Carson

But their time at Bosque Redondo was even worse. Bad river water made them sick. They planted crops, but nothing grew. Supplies often arrived late or failed to arrive at all. Disease, harsh weather, and malnutrition overcame them. During four ghastly years at Bosque Redondo, more than a quarter of the Navajos perished. They call that period Nahonzod—the Fearing Time.

Two of the Navajos who suffered at Bosque Redondo

By the summer of 1863, the North seemed to be winning the Civil War. Union victories at Gettysburg and Vicksburg had turned the Confederate tide. Yet for all the battles back East, there had been few civilian casualties. Out West, however, it was a different story.

In Kansas and Missouri, both sides waged devastating guerrilla warfare, targeting innocent civilians as well as rival armies. The most infamous Confederate guerrillas were led by William Quantrill and "Bloody Bill" Anderson. Quantrill was a former

William Quantrill (left)
and "Bloody Bill" Anderson

schoolteacher from Ohio with little interest in slavery but limitless enthusiasm for looting and killing. Anderson wore a necklace of Yankee scalps into battle and laughed as unarmed prisoners were gunned down.

On the morning of August 21, 1863, Quantrill, Anderson, and 450 men rode toward an unsuspecting town. It was Lawrence, still the antislavery stronghold of Kansas, and the target once more of an army of ruffians. Julia Louisa Lovejoy lived in a little house nearby. Her husband was in the East, with the Union army.

I could see every house this side of Lawrence, with a volume of dense smoke arising from them as they advanced, firing every house in their march of death.

—Julia Louisa Lovejoy

"I rushed out and saw the smoke," she wrote. "I could see every house this side of Lawrence, with a volume of dense smoke arising from them as they advanced, firing every house in their march of death."

The raiders stormed into town and began destroying it. While Quantrill ate a leisurely breakfast, Anderson and his men carried out his deadly orders. Hotels, banks, and businesses, as well as nearly two hundred

A painting depicts Quantrill's raid on Lawrence, Kansas.

homes, were plundered, then burned. Some 183 men and boys were killed. Fewer than twenty had been soldiers. The guerrillas threw the dead and dying into the raging fires.

"One lady threw her arms around her husband and begged them to spare his life," Mrs. Lovejoy wrote. "They rested the pistol on her arm as it was around his body, and shot him dead, and the fire from the pistol burnt the sleeve of her dress."

Julia Lovejoy and her young son hid in the tall weeds. Their house was spared when Quantrill's raiders took a different road out of Lawrence, leaving behind eighty widows and 250 fatherless children.

To avenge the Lawrence massacre, federal troops forced every family in three Missouri counties from their homes and out onto the open prairie. Union guerrillas burned and looted the empty houses left behind and raided the helpless columns of refugees.

Three of Quantrill's raiders. Guerrilla fighters on both sides brought the Civil War's bloodshed to innocent civilians.

By the time it was all over, thousands had died in Kansas and Missouri in the most cold-blooded killing of the war. "The very air seems charged with blood and death," a Kansas newspaper reported. "Death runs riot over the country."

For some, however, the West was a haven from the Civil War. In the mining camps, work went on as usual, even in places crowded with prospectors from both North and South. Congress authorized the start of a transcontinental railroad and passed the Homestead Act, offering free land to anyone who worked it for five years. Thousands of young men decided they would rather go west than go to battle.

Sam Clemens, age twenty-four, was one of them. Two weeks in the Confederate militia convinced him that he was not cut out for combat. In 1861, he and his brother took the overland stagecoach to Nevada. There, Clemens tried his hand at everything he could think of to make a fortune. Nothing worked.

He bought some forest land near Lake Tahoe, dreaming of becoming a lumber king. But he was careless with a cooking fire and watched his forest burn. He spent six months in a small cabin with three partners, prospecting for silver, dreaming of riches—and going deeper into debt. "We were stark mad with excitement, drunk with happiness, smothered under mountains of prospective wealth," he wrote, "but our credit was not good at the grocer's." He would later boast that he became a multimillionaire for just ten days—until fourteen armed men jumped his claim.

Sam Clemens

Then Clemens talked himself into a job as a newspaper reporter in Virginia City, Nevada. He covered everything from shoot-outs to theatrical performances, but people seemed to enjoy his humorous articles the best. "It is nothing to be proud of," he wrote to his mother, "but it is my strongest suit."

In the West, while sitting out the war, Sam Clemens had finally found his calling. He began to sign his articles with a new pen name—Mark Twain.

Early in the war, President Lincoln had called some Cheyenne chiefs to the White House to ask them not to side with the Confederacy. The chiefs assured him that their people wanted no part of the conflict

and went home to the plains wearing peace medals the president had given them.

But in the end, like many other tribes, the Cheyenne could not escape the war. After the Colorado gold rush, they had signed a treaty ceding much of their land to the United States, except for a small reservation southeast of Denver, along a small stream called Sand Creek. The treaty proved to be a bad bargain. The area had little game to hunt, and supplies that had been promised did not arrive. Some Cheyenne were reduced to begging white settlers for food. Others began raiding and destroying ranches.

Throughout the summer of 1864, there was killing on both sides—Indians shot down and settlers murdered. That fall, a group of Cheyenne chiefs came to Denver to arrange a peace. Among them was Black Kettle, one of the tribe's most respected leaders.

As a young man, Black Kettle had led war parties against the Kiowas, Utes, and Delawares, and fought white soldiers in Kansas. Now he was a "peace chief." Following a tradition laid down many years earlier by the

Cheyenne prophet Sweet Medicine, peace chiefs were selected for their wisdom and generosity and were expected to look after their people's welfare. Black Kettle believed that the best way for the Cheyenne to survive was to avoid fighting the whites.

The sky has been dark ever since the war began. We want to take good tidings home to our people, that they may sleep in peace.

— *Black Kettle*

"I want all these chiefs of the soldiers here to understand that we are for peace, that we may not be mistaken for enemies," Black Kettle told the army officers and governor of Colorado Territory. As proof of his good faith, he turned over four white captives he had ransomed from other Cheyenne bands. Assured that his people would be safe, Black Kettle agreed they would return to Sand Creek.

Black Kettle's peace delegation arrives in Denver.

But not all the soldiers wanted peace—especially John Chivington, the hero of Glorieta Pass, who now hoped to advance his political career with a victory over the Indians. His new troops, the Third Colorado Volunteers, were being scorned by newspapers as "the Bloodless Third" and were itching for a fight.

At dawn on November 29, 1864, Chivington and seven hundred men reached the edge of Black Kettle's sleeping village on the banks of Sand Creek. An American flag and a white flag flew over Black Kettle's tepee. Chivington ordered an attack anyway, though some officers refused to take part.

Some two hundred Cheyenne—men, women, children, even babies—were killed that morning, their bodies scalped and then mutilated. White Antelope, an aging chief who was wearing the peace medal President Lincoln had given him, was one of the first to fall.

Most army officers were sickened by what Chivington and his volunteers had done. General Ulysses S. Grant considered the massacre nothing less than murder. Both Congress and the U.S. army launched investigations and denounced Chivington, but by the time they reached their verdicts, he was a civilian again and beyond the reach of military justice.

Black Kettle was among those who escaped the slaughter. He led the survivors south, seeking to avoid further bloodshed.

John M. Chivington

On April 9, 1865, Robert E. Lee surrendered his Confederate army at Appomattox Courthouse, in Virginia. The Civil War was over. But in parts of the West, it continued to sputter on.

A month later, the final skirmish of the war was fought—at Palmito Ranch, in Texas. And several weeks after that, Brigadier General Stand Watie, a Cherokee, turned himself and his Indian troops over to federal officials. He was the last Southern general to surrender.

The newly reunited nation now turned its attention to the West as never before. Work on a transcontinental railroad resumed. Hundreds of thousands of settlers, many of them war veterans, rushed west to start new lives. But standing in their path were the Indians of the plains—the Arapahos, Kiowas, Comanches, Lakotas, and Cheyenne, many of whom had vowed to fight the encroachment of white people after the massacre at Sand Creek.

The government sent its most celebrated officers to subdue them. But the heroes of the Civil War in the East soon ran into trouble trying to conquer the Indians of the West. In Wyoming, the Lakotas wiped out an entire command of eighty soldiers led by Lieutenant William J. Fetterman. General Winfield Scott Hancock, who had held back the Confederate charge at Gettysburg, spent four frustrating months trying to drive the Cheyenne and Arapahos from Nebraska and Kansas. During that time, his men killed two Indians, while the roaming Indian bands raided and killed two hundred settlers.

George Armstrong Custer, dressed for the winter campaign against the Cheyenne

George Armstrong Custer, one of the Union's most famous generals, also did poorly. His cavalry chased Lakota and Cheyenne warriors all across the plains. They couldn't catch any of them. Instead, in one surprise attack, the Lakotas stole several of Custer's favorite horses.

The army finally decided to use the same military strategy that had brought the South to its knees—breaking the enemies' ability and will to resist by destroying their homes and food supplies. It was called "total war."

General Philip Sheridan had used the strategy in Virginia's Shenandoah Valley, stripping farms of crops and livestock. General William Tecumseh Sherman had done the same through Georgia, where the blackened chimneys of hundreds of buildings between Atlanta and the sea proved the theory's effectiveness. Now they would apply similar tactics in the West, wherever Indians continued to resist. Winter, they decided, would be the best time.

Three separate columns of troops rode out to sweep through the southern plains and force the Cheyenne onto a reservation. At the head of one of them rode Custer, who pushed his men relentlessly through driving snow and bitter winds.

One night, Custer's Indian scouts reported they had followed the pony tracks of a raiding party to a Cheyenne village near the Washita River in what is now Oklahoma. Custer ordered his men to prepare for a dawn attack, although he didn't know how many Indians were there or whose village it was.

As it happened, it was Black Kettle's.

"I have always done my best to keep my young men quiet," he had told a government official earlier, "but some will not listen, and since the fight-

General William Tecumseh Sherman (third from left) proposed "total war" against the South — and then against the Indians.

ing began [after Sand Creek] I have not been able to keep them all at home. But we want peace." It was some of those young men's pony tracks that had led Custer and his troops to the edge of Black Kettle's village.

November 27, 1868, dawned—two days short of the fourth anniversary of the slaughter at Sand Creek. Once again, Black Kettle was awakened by the noises of a cavalry attack—the thunder of hooves, the blare of trumpets, and the sharp cracks of rifle shots. He and his wife jumped onto his pony as Custer and six hundred troops charged into the village.

During the Battle of Washita, nearly forty Cheyenne died, less than half of them warriors. Custer lost twenty-one men. But he took fifty-three prisoners, captured nearly nine hundred Indian horses, and destroyed more than fifty Cheyenne lodges, along with the village's buffalo robes, equipment, and winter food supplies. Black Kettle and his wife were among the dead.

•◆•

Native Americans were most vulnerable to attack during winter.

On the southern plains, the relentless winter campaign succeeded for the army. One by one, tribes facing starvation or destruction surrendered, although farther north the Lakotas and some other bands still resisted.

They told [Custer] then that if ever afterward he should break that peace promise and should fight the Cheyennes, the Everywhere Spirit surely would cause him to be killed.
— Kate Bighead, Cheyenne survivor of Washita

In the spring of 1869, the last southern Cheyenne holdouts turned themselves in to Custer. He met in the tepee of a chief named Rock Forehead, who sat the general down under the sacred arrows, the Cheyenne's most honored and powerful relics, given to them by Sweet Medicine so many years before.

Custer smoked a peace pipe with Rock Forehead. But when they finished, the chief tapped out the ashes onto the officer's boots—to bring Custer bad luck and drive home a warning. If he ever broke his peace promise and fought the Cheyenne again, Custer was told, the "Everywhere Spirit" watching over them would make sure he died.

The Grandest Enterprise
Under God
1868-1874

By 1868, crews made up of immigrants had been struggling for five years to build a railroad that would at last link the Atlantic and Pacific Oceans. Many Americans believed that the completion of a transcontinental railroad would finally unite the nation, East and West, just as the Civil War's end had reunited the North and South.

But the railroad would do far more than that. Like the arrival of the horse two centuries earlier, railroads would transform the West—only at a much faster pace.

Railroads would connect eastern cities with hundreds of thousands of Texas cattle, and the dusty, saddle-sore men who herded them would suddenly become heroes in the eyes of eastern schoolchildren.

Railroads would allow millions of freedom-seeking homesteaders from around the world to start new towns on the open prairie and plant crops in soil that had never known anything but grass.

And railroads would bring onto the Great Plains the buffalo hunters, who would drive a magnificent animal that symbolized the West and sustained its native peoples to the brink of extinction.

•◆• •◆• •◆•

For a quarter of a century, Americans had dreamed of building a railroad linking coast to coast. Now, at last, it was being built — 1,775 miles of track from Omaha, Nebraska, to Sacramento, California.

The great Pacific Railway is commenced.... This is the grandest enterprise under God!

— George Francis Train, railroad promoter

No one had ever before undertaken such a task. The railroad would have to cut through mountains higher than any railroad builder had ever faced, span deserts where there was no water for the crews, and cross treeless prairies where Indians would resist its passage. If it could be completed, the railroad across the West would be one of the greatest engineering projects the world had ever seen.

"The great Pacific Railway is commenced," exclaimed George Francis Train, an aptly named railroad promoter. "This is the grandest enterprise under God!"

Two companies had won government contracts for the job. The Central Pacific pushed eastward from Sacramento, over the high, steep mountains of the Sierra Nevada. The Union Pacific started at the Missouri River, heading west over the Great Plains toward

Union Pacific crews headed west from Omaha.

the Rocky Mountains. Each company would get thousands of dollars and 6,400 acres of federal land for each mile of track it laid. A race soon developed to see which company could cover the most ground before the two lines met.

In Nebraska, some ten thousand men worked for the Union Pacific. Most had emigrated from Ireland, but there were also Mexicans, Germans, Englishmen, ex–Civil War soldiers, and former slaves.

They rose at down in a twenty-car work train and started a day of backbreaking labor. There was no heavy machinery in those days; everything was done by hand. Advance crews used shovels to build a level path. Others carried sturdy wooden timbers, called ties, and laid them across the roadbed. Then the "iron men" lifted the rails (each one weighed seven hundred pounds) and put them on the ties. The next crew swung heavy sledgehammers to drive in spikes, while others bolted on connecting

The Central Pacific pushed eastward from Sacramento.

plates to hold the rails in place. Finally a tamping crew smoothed the roadbed out again. By nightfall, they had laid only two or three miles of track.

An Englishman named William Bell traveled west to report on the railroad's progress and marveled at the scene: "It is a Grand Anvil Chorus that these sturdy sledges are playing across the plains. It is in triple time, three strokes to a spike. Twenty-one million times are they to come down, before the great work of modern America is complete."

We saw the first train of cars that any of us had seen. Far off it was very small, but it kept coming and growing larger all the time, puffing out smoke and steam; and as it came on, we said to each other that it looked like a white man's pipe when he was smoking.

— *Porcupine, northern Cheyenne*

Not everyone was as impressed by the Union Pacific's work. The Plains Indian tribes resented what they called the "metal road" and the "iron horse" that followed it. The railroad cut through their lands. Union Pacific hunters shot thousands of buffalo to feed the hungry crews. New towns sprang up with each advance of the rail line. "As we talked of our troubles," a northern

The railroad cut through the heart of Indian lands.

Cheyenne named Porcupine remembered, "we said among ourselves: Now the white people have taken all we had and have made us poor, and we ought to do something."

Along the route, bands of northern Cheyenne, Arapahos, and Lakotas fired on the workers, and even derailed a train and ransacked its freight cars. Finally five thousand U.S. army troops were sent west to protect the workers and keep construction moving forward.

Meanwhile, in California, the Central Pacific was stuck in the Sierra Nevada. The towering mountains seemed insurmountable. To make matters worse, three out of every five workers had abandoned their railroad jobs to look for gold and silver in Nevada.

In desperation, Charles Crocker, the company's construction boss, decided to hire Chinese laborers. Some people warned that the Chinese were too small, too inexperienced, and too "different" for the job. When Crocker hired a test crew of fifty Chinese men, doubters scoffed and

Chinese workers on the Central Pacific

called them "Crocker's pets." But they proved to be efficient, hard workers. Before long, eleven thousand Chinese were on the payroll—and the Central Pacific was back in the race.

To conquer the Sierras, the Chinese crews used five hundred kegs of blasting powder a day. They cut down giant redwood trees by hand and carved ledges across sheer cliffs more than two thousand feet above raging rivers. They drilled and blasted out fifteen tunnels through solid granite, sometimes working in shifts around the clock to move ahead only eight inches in one day. When heavy snows began falling, they kept working, living in tunnels under snowdrifts forty feet deep. Some men froze to death; others were swept away by avalanches. Before it was over, more than 1,200 Chinese would die building the railroad.

In early 1868, the Central Pacific broke out of the mountains and onto the Nevada deserts. Here the crews suffered from lack of water, scorpions, cholera, and summer temperatures of 120 degrees. Still, the Chinese pushed on.

Railways, multiplied and spanning the continent, are ... more powerful and more permanent than law ... or political constitutions. — William Gilpin

By the spring of 1869, the competition between the Central Pacific and Union Pacific was converging on Utah. No fixed meeting point had ever been established, so government engineers picked Promontory Summit, fifty-six miles west of Ogden. The race across the West was coming to a close.

By May 10, everything was ready for the two lines to join. A crew of Chinese workers brought up a rail for the Central Pacific, while the Union Pacific's Irishmen placed one down for their company. Four spikes—two gold, one silver, and the fourth a blend of gold, silver, and iron—were tapped gently into place. The fifth and final spike was connected to a telegrapher's key to signal both coasts and all points in between that the great project was at last complete.

Leland Stanford, president of the Central Pacific, swung a silver-headed sledgehammer down. He missed. The telegrapher sent the signal anyway: "DONE!"

On May 10, 1869, the two lines finally met at Promontory Summit.

In Washington, D.C., a great cheer went up and an illuminated ball dropped from the dome of the Capitol. At Independence Hall in Philadelphia, the Liberty Bell was rung—gingerly, so that its crack would not widen. And in San Francisco, a huge celebration began.

The vast distances of the West had finally been conquered. A journey that had once taken months could now be accomplished in a matter of days. Engraved on the official spike was a special prayer: "May God continue the unity of our Country as this Railroad unites the two great Oceans of the world."

•◆•

Charles Goodnight

Cattle had first entered the West with Coronado in 1540. And long before the United States expanded beyond the Mississippi, Spanish and Mexican *ranchos* had established the cattle business and its distinctive customs—from the roundup to branding irons, from the boots on a vaquero's feet to the leather chaps on his legs, the lasso in his hands, and the wide-brimmed hat on his head.

Now, as more railroads began spreading across the West, beef could finally be easily shipped to markets in crowded eastern cities—but only if the cattle could get to the railroads.

One of the first to figure out how to get them there was Charles Goodnight. He had grown up poor, a farmer's son from Illinois. At age nine, Goodnight rode bareback all the way to Texas, and he had been working full-time to support his widowed mother since he was eleven. At nineteen he began building his own cattle herd by taking care of someone else's and receiving every fourth calf as pay. He was barely thirty when he and Oliver Loving blazed the Goodnight-Loving trail from Texas, where there were plenty of cattle but little money after the Civil War, to better markets in New Mexico, Colorado, and Wyoming. They cleared twenty-four thousand dollars on their first trip.

I never had a compass in my life. I was never lost.

—*Charles Goodnight*

Over the next nine years, sometimes making two trail drives in one season, Goodnight personally moved one hundred thousand cattle out of Texas. He was seen as a pioneer in the business—"Old Charlie," they called him, though he was not yet forty.

He could read the signs of nature to find water for his herds and his men. Swallows flying low and straight, he said, were headed toward water. A piece of copper, placed in your mouth, he added, helped ward off severe thirst; a peeled slice of prickly pear cactus was even better. Newborn calves, he learned, slowed down a trail drive, so he placed them in a wagon every morning, wrapping them in burlap bags so they would keep their own scent and their mothers could find them when they were turned loose every night. And he redesigned an old wagon for the trail drive's cook, a kind of kitchen on wheels called the chuck wagon.

Soon, there were other trails—the Shawnee, the Western, and the Chisholm. In less than twenty years, some six million steers and cows moved along them; so many that in places the dust was knee-deep. At

After the roundup, the herds were driven toward the nearest railroad.

first, the men who herded them were called drovers. It was considered a much more respectable term than *cow-boy*, which originally referred to young men on horseback who stole someone else's cattle. But as the trail drive era hit its peak in the 1870s, eastern writers began to romanticize life on the open prairie. The cowboy was transformed into a symbol of the "Wild West"—a man who spent most of his time in fighting Indians and outlaws and not much working with cattle.

ROUNDUP SCENES AT BELLE FOURCHE IN 1887. PHOTOGRAPHED BY GRABILL - STURGIS. D.T.

Cowboys ate their meals outdoors…

and bathed outdoors, too.

The reality was quite different. Trail drives lasted four months or more. Every day the herd had to be moved—slowly, so the cattle would not lose weight. Twelve to fifteen miles a day was a good pace. The days were dusty and long. "The men slept on the ground with their horses staked nearby," Goodnight remembered. "Sometimes the demands were so urgent that our boots were not taken off for an entire week." The food was monotonous, usually beans and hard bread. Trail bosses like Charles Goodnight prohibited drinking, gambling, and gunplay.

Few cowboys died at the hands of Indians and outlaws. Drowning at a river crossing was a bigger fear, since few of them could swim. But the most common way that cowboys died on

the trail was by being dragged to death, so the most dreaded moment was a nighttime stampede. "The cattle were nervous and easily frightened, and the slightest noise might startle them into running," Goodnight said. "The heat developed by a large drove of cattle during a stampede was surprising, and the odor given off by the clashing horns and hooves was nearly overpowering.... Animal heat seems to attract electricity, especially when the cattle are wet, and after a storm I have seen the faces of men riding with a herd scorched as if some furnace blast had blazed against them."

The men slept on the ground with their horses staked nearby. Sometimes the demands were so urgent that our boots were not taken off for an entire week.

—Charles Goodnight

The cowboys' average age was twenty-four. Roughly a third of them were Mexicans or African Americans. (Goodnight's most trusted cowboy was Bose Ikard, a former slave.) They owned their saddles but not the

Many cowboys were Mexican Americans…

or former slaves.

horses they rode. And with a wage of only thirty dollars a month, a cattle drive bought them little more than new clothes—and perhaps one wild weekend at trail's end in a railroad town like Abilene, Wichita, or Dodge City. The work was so hard and the pay so low that only one out of three cowboys ever went on a second trail drive.

"Old Charlie" Goodnight was an exception. Few men made as many trail drives as he did. "All in all, my years on the trail were the happiest I ever lived," he said. "There were many hardships and dangers, of course, but most of the time we were solitary adventurers in a great land as fresh and new as a spring morning, and we were free and full of the zest of darers."

In the midst of the Civil War, Congress had passed the Homestead Act, which promised 160 acres of public land to any person who paid a ten-dollar fee and worked the property for five years. Railroad companies, too, were given millions of acres in government subsidies and offered them for sale.

Now, with railroads to carry them, settlers flooded west in numbers unimaginable only a few years earlier. Some 4.5 million arrived in the 1870s. Most of them came from states along the Mississippi River, which actually lost population for a few years. But settlers came from Europe as well. For them, the prospect of 160 acres of unbroken soil in a land without kings and queens seemed like a dream come true.

"There are three Norwegian settlements here with approximately three hundred inhabitants, including eight Danes and one Swede," an immigrant named Elise Waerenskjold wrote home to Norway from her homestead on the plains. "Most of the people were poor when they came, but all of them have prospered, more or less. Families can be found who were in debt when they arrived, but are now well off…because land is cheap."

Two hundred Scottish families settled on the Kansas-Nebraska border. The Hebrew Immigrant Aid Society helped Jews from eastern Europe to settle in Oregon, Colorado, and the Dakotas. Dutch, French, Bohemian, and Irish families were soon scattered across the prairies.

Some English aristocrats bought fifty thousand acres from the Kansas Pacific Railroad and started their own community. They held "fox hunts" in the mornings—chasing coyotes on horseback—played cricket in the afternoons, and held banquets and balls in the evening. "Even with plenty

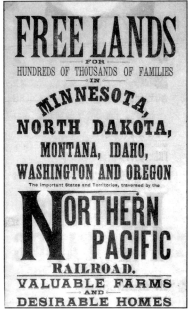

Railroads advertised for more settlers.

For these English aristocrats in Kansas, "pioneering" included tennis.

of money," one of them remembered, "it was still pioneering." Within a few years, most of them had given up and returned to England.

Mennonites, Catholics, Hutterites, and Amish people fled persecution in

The greatest curse to a new country, and indeed, to all countries, is to have large tracts of unoccupied lands.... I am for opening these lands for the landless of every nation under heaven.

—Senator Samuel Pomeroy, Kansas

Russia and started over in Kansas, where they built villages with the same names, same street plans, and same types of homes they had left behind. They were the world's best wheat farmers, and the seeds they brought with them from the Russian steppes flourished on

the western plains. Mixed in with the wheat came a weed that adapted just as successfully, a plant that spread so fast that it became a symbol of the American West: the russian thistle, better known as the tumbleweed.

German-Russian settlers in Montana

78

Regardless of where they came from, the new westerners faced the same challenges, opportunities, and hardships. They went immediately to work turning the thick, rich soil that had never before been plowed—it sounded like a giant zipper opening when the first plow blade ran across it, some said—and planting their crops. With virtually no trees in sight, small houses called soddies were built of dirt bricks; others, called dugouts, were carved out of hillsides like caves. "Our first home was a dugout," Berna Chrisman remembered of her childhood. "Fleas, rattlesnakes, and coyotes were galore, but of all these the fleas were the greatest pest, for they were always with us, day and night." Young Walter Posey was constantly awakened in the night by salamanders in his family's dirt house. They were, he said, "just about as cold as a dog's nose when he smells you."

Children were expected to do their share of the homestead labor. They gathered dried buffalo dung for fuel, fetched water, weeded gardens, milked cows, and fed chickens, and at harvesttime labored in the fields with their parents. "Sometimes I would lie down on my sack and want to die," Edna Matthews Clifton said of her youth on a frontier farm. "Sometimes they would pour water over my head to relieve me. [But] it was

Within the image: 36 Independence on the Plains   Gathering Chips.

Gathering buffalo dung for fuel in Kansas

instilled in us that work was necessary. Everybody worked; it was a part of life, for there was no life without it."

There were prairie fires, tornadoes, droughts, freezing winters, and spring floods to contend with. In 1874, and again in 1876, plagues of grasshoppers arrived in swarms so thick and huge that they darkened the midday sky and then devoured everything in their path. "Water troughs and loosely covered wells were foul with drowned 'hoppers," said William Meredith. "A young wife awaiting her first baby, in the absence of her husband, went insane from fright, all alone in that sun-baked shanty on the bald prairie."

Some homesteaders gave up and returned home, or moved on to start again somewhere else in the West. But enough stayed on — and so many more continued to arrive — that by the end of the 1870s, the populations of Kansas, Nebraska, Colorado, and the Dakotas had more than tripled in a decade.

Everybody worked; it was part of life, for there was no life without it.

— *Edna Matthews Clifton, daughter of homesteaders*

In 1872, a twenty-two-year-old from Louisiana named Frank Mayer arrived in Dodge City, Kansas, a new town created by the Atchison, Topeka and Santa Fe railroad. He was looking for work and excitement when he met two buffalo hunters who offered to show him their trade. "I was young [and] I needed adventure," he later remembered. "Here was it."

At the time, there was great demand in the East for buffalo products—especially buffalo hides, which could be made into leather for shoes, carriage tops, and the wide belts that turned machinery in eastern factories. The new rail lines reaching into buffalo country could now ship in more hunters and ship out more hides than ever before.

Frank Mayer

The buffalo, Mayer believed, "were walking gold pieces.... Just think. There were twenty million buffalo, each worth at least three dollars.... I could kill a hundred a day. That would be $6,000 a month—or three times what was paid the President of the United States."

Mayer sank everything he owned into a hunting outfit—wagons, mules, camp equipment, rifles, and ammunition—and headed out onto the plains, expecting to make a fortune.

But he was not alone. Some two thousand other men came to Dodge City that same year with the same plan. In the town's first three months of existence, it shipped east 43,029 buffalo hides and 1.4 million pounds of buffalo meat.

The buffalo didn't belong to anybody. If you could kill them, what they brought was yours. They were walking gold pieces.

— *Frank Mayer*

Mayer and the others called themselves buffalo runners, not hunters, but they avoided running—or even riding—after buffalo as much as possible. For efficiency's sake, the mounted buffalo chase gave way to

A buffalo herd on the move

A hunter with his kill

a technique called the stand. First, the hunters placed themselves upwind from a herd (so the animals couldn't detect them by their smell). Then, with their powerful long-range rifles, they shot the lead buffalo. As the rest of the herd began to mill around its body, the hunters would methodically shoot the others, one by one. They stopped only when their rifles overheated or when they had killed so many buffalo that the skinners could not get all their hides.

"Adventurous?" Mayer recalled. "No more than shooting a beef critter in the barnyard. It was a harvest. We were the harvesters, we businessmen with rifles."

Buffalo skeletons, bleached by the sun, soon covered the prairies—and started still another industry. Buffalo horns could be turned into buttons, combs, and knife handles. Hooves could be rendered into glue. Bones could be ground into fertilizer. Homesteaders and professional "bone pickers" gathered the skeletons and brought them to railroad sidings. Some 32 million pounds of buffalo bones made their way to eastern factories in just three years.

Some Americans grew alarmed at the extent of the slaughter. Bills were proposed in Congress and state legislatures to stop it, but they never became law. General Phil Sheridan and others argued instead that eliminating the great buffalo herds was the fastest way to force Indian tribes into submission. Without the buffalo, he said, they would have to rely on farming and government rations on reservations for their food.

But the buffalo meant much more than food to the Indians. "Everything the Kiowas had came from the buffalo," said a woman named Old Lady Horse, expressing the customs of many western tribes. "Their tepees were made of buffalo hides, so were their clothes and moccasins. . . . Their containers were made of hide, or of bladders or stomachs. . . . Most of all the buffalo was part of the Kiowa religion. The priests used parts of the buffalo to make their prayers when they healed people or when they sang to the powers above. The buffalo were the *life* of the Kiowas."

*Carting buffalo bones
to a railroad*

The end of the line: buffalo bones stacked near an eastern factory

In the summer of 1874, the Kiowas and other tribes on the southern plains rose up to drive out the hunters. But Sheridan's troops forced them all to surrender and report to reservations. The buffalo hunters went back to work. Within a few years, the southern herd had disappeared. Later, when railroads finally penetrated the northern plains, the same thing happened there.

*O*ne by one we…put up our buffalo rifles [and] left the ranges. And there settled over them a vast quiet. The buffalo was gone.

— Frank Mayer

Once an estimated thirty million or more buffalo had roamed the West. By the turn of the century, there would be fewer than one hundred.

A Crow medicine woman named Pretty-Shield remembered the impact of the buffalo's slaughter. "When the buffalo went away," she said, "the hearts of my people fell to the ground, and they could not lift them up again."

Fight No More Forever
1874-1877

By 1874, railroads were opening up new opportunities to millions of newcomers in the West. But the "iron horse" was also changing forever the lives of Indian peoples who had called the West home for hundreds of generations.

The buffalo were disappearing, and in their place came homesteads, new towns, and herds of cattle. Nearly every tribe that once resisted the American transformation of the West had been forced to surrender.

But some bands still held out. Between 1874 and 1877, they would make a last stand to remain free. One would be led by a Lakota medicine man who saw the Americans as his worst enemies. Another would follow a Nez Percé chief who had always considered the Americans his good friends.

To subdue the Indians, the government would rely on an unlikely army that was accustomed more to boredom than to fighting—but that also included a dashing and impulsive young general who came west pursuing a vision of his own invincibility, only to meet an enemy whose visions proved even stronger.

•◆• •◆• •◆•

Some Indians called Custer "Yellow Hair."

In the summer of 1874, a column of one thousand soldiers marched out of Fort Abraham Lincoln, in Dakota Territory, and headed southwest, straight into the Black Hills. At the head of the expedition rode one of the army's most celebrated officers, George Armstrong Custer.

An Ohio blacksmith's son who graduated at the bottom of his class at West Point, Custer had nonetheless become a hero of the Civil War. In battle after battle, he had led daring cavalry charges against the Confederates. Eleven horses had been shot out from under him. At the age of twenty-three, he had become the youngest general in the Union Army.

Custer was as flamboyant as he was fearless. When he came west and took command of the Seventh Cavalry after the war, he brought along some thoroughbred horses and a pack of staghounds for hunting, and he designed for himself a distinctive costume made of buckskins, meant to catch the notice of visiting newspaper reporters. He wore his curly golden hair down to his shoulders. (The Cheyenne especially admired it and began to call him "Yellow Hair.")

Oh, could you have but seen some of the charges we made! While thinking of them I cannot but exclaim, "Glorious War!"

— *George Armstrong Custer*

He even wrote a book about himself, glorifying his exploits.

But the honor and fame Custer assumed he would win against the Indians eluded him at first. His soldiers chased Lakota and Cheyenne warriors for months but couldn't catch any. Some of his troops deserted. While riding after a buffalo one day, Custer somehow shot his own horse in the head in midgallop. On foot, bruised from the fall, and totally lost, he had to be rescued by his men. And after abandoning his command to ride across Kansas and see his wife, Custer was court-martialed and temporarily suspended from service.

Custer's expedition heads toward the Black Hills.

But his surprise attack on Black Kettle's Cheyenne village at Washita in 1868 had redeemed his reputation with his superiors—and the public.

Now Custer and the Seventh Cavalry had ridden into the heart of the Black Hills, an area the Lakotas considered sacred ground and a place few white men had ever been. There, some of his men found gold.

The discovery made Custer even more famous—and set off a gold rush. Some fifteen thousand whites swarmed in. Half a dozen towns sprang up, including one named for Custer.

All of this activity violated the Fort Laramie Treaty of 1868, signed by the Lakotas and the United States after years of deadly and expensive warfare on the northern plains. In the treaty, the Lakotas agreed to stop raiding settlers and attacking army units and to stay within the boundaries of a large reservation. In exchange, the United States promised schools, food, and supplies and vowed that much of South Dakota would be the Lakotas' forever.

To the Lakotas, the Black Hills were especially important. Their valleys sheltered many game animals, and their slopes were covered with trees for fuel—ideal for winter camp. And although the Lakotas themselves had once driven other tribes out of the area, they now considered the Black Hills sacred to their people.

By treaty, the U.S. army was expected to remove the prospectors, but there were far too many. Instead, the government offered to buy the gold region from the Indians for six million dollars. The Lakotas turned it down.

The prospectors called Custer's path into the Black Hills the Freedom Trail. The Lakotas called it the Thieves' Road.

The Lakotas had many leaders—Black Moon, Rain-in-the-Face, Gall, Crazy Horse. But the man to whom even these veteran fighters now looked for guidance was Sitting Bull, a chief and medicine man determined never to give up the Black Hills.

He had counted coup (touched an enemy in battle) by age fourteen, during a raid on the Crows. As leader of the Strong Heart warrior society, he had won battles against the Crows, Assiniboins, and Shoshones—victories his followers credited to the extraordinary power of his mystical visions.

I will remain what I am until I die, a hunter, and when there are no buffalo or other game I will send my children to hunt and live on prairie mice.

—Sitting Bull

No one had earned a greater reputation for bravery. Once, in the midst of a fight with U.S. soldiers on the Yellowstone River, he strolled out between the lines and calmly sat down. Then, with bullets pattering all around him, he filled his pipe and smoked it slowly until the bowl was empty.

And no one was more opposed to giving up the old ways for life on the reservation. "Look at me!" he once told a band of Assiniboins, "See if *I* am poor, or my people either. The whites may get me at last, as you say, but I will have good times till then. You are fools to make yourselves slaves to a piece of fat bacon . . . and a little sugar and coffee."

Sitting Bull's name—Tatanka Iyotanka—was meant to describe a powerful buffalo of great endurance, one that never budged when attacked and instead planted its feet and fought to the death.

Sitting Bull and other defiant Lakota chiefs had refused to even discuss the possible sale of the Black Hills. "I want to hunt in this place," he said. "I want you to turn back from here. I want you to leave what you have got here and turn back. If you don't, I'll fight you."

Many whites also saw no alternative but war. "The American people need the country the Indians now occupy," wrote the *Bismarck Tribune*. "Many of our people are out of employment [and] the masses need some new

Sitting Bull

excitement. An Indian war would do no harm, for it must come, sooner or later."

General Phil Sheridan ordered all Lakotas to report to reservation headquarters. When Sitting Bull and the others refused, Sheridan began to plan a military campaign to force them in.

An Indian war would do no harm, for it must come, sooner or later. —BISMARCK TRIBUNE

In the years following the Civil War, the U.S. army was assigned an impossible task in the West. With fewer than fifteen thousand men (sometimes as few as three thousand) scattered among one hundred forts and outposts, it was told to police 2.5 million square miles of land. Somehow, the army was expected to defend settlers, ranchers, miners, and railroad crews, keep tens of thousands of Indians confined to their reservations, *and* keep tens of thousands of whites off of Indian lands.

New recruits at Forth Keogh, Montana

Pay was low—just thirteen dollars a month. Army ranks filled with immigrants, some of whom could not speak English, as well as drifters and men escaping bad marriages or the law, who often enlisted under assumed names.

Four regiments were made up of African Americans, for whom serving in the army was one of the few careers available at the time. They were segregated from the other troops, but they fought in nearly two hundred battles and won seventeen Medals of Honor for bravery. The Indians thought their hair resembled that of the buffalo and called them "buffalo soldiers," a term the men proudly adopted for themselves.

"Buffalo soldiers" at Fort Wingate, New Mexico

For all soldiers, discipline was severe. Men were flogged for minor offenses, locked up in stockades, or suspended by their thumbs. Sometimes the food was inedible—stale Civil War rations so hard they had to

Some soldiers were disciplined on a wooden "punishment horse," where they were forced to sit for hours, holding a heavy wooden saber.

be shattered with a hammer or "Cincinnati Chicken," a mixture of bacon and salt pork that was dipped in vinegar and eaten raw.

On the northern plains, winters were unbearably long and cold. In the Southwest, soldiers routinely marched across deserts in 120-degree heat. "Everything dries," J. Ross Brown wrote from Fort Yuma in Arizona. "Men dry;

Some of what are called military posts are... about as much forts as prairie dog villages might be called forts. —*General William Tecumseh Sherman*

chickens dry; there is not juice left in anything, living or dead, by the close of summer. Chickens hatched at this season, as old Fort Yumers say, come out of the shell already cooked."

Most army regulars never met an Indian in battle. Some never saw any Indians at all. Boredom was the only thing they could depend upon, three to five years of it. They quarreled, drank, even pitted red ants against black ants just to stir things up. Many deserted, giving the army the "grand bounce." Nearly 8 percent committed suicide.

Disease was the worst killer. In two years, Custer's Seventh Cavalry, one of the most active units, lost thirty-six men to Indians and six men to drowning, while two were declared missing in action; during the same period, fifty-one men died from cholera.

Then came the year 1876.

That spring, Sitting Bull climbed to a hilltop, seeking a vision. In his dream, a great whirlwind of dust collided with a small white cloud that resembled a Lakota village. Through the whirlwind, Sitting Bull could see soldiers marching. Then the storm passed, and the cloud remained. It meant, he said, that the Indians would be attacked but win a great victory.

At the time, three army units had been dispatched to drive the defiant Lakota bands onto the reservation. One was moving north from Wyoming and another east from western Montana. The third was the Seventh Cavalry, 566 enlisted men and 31 officers marching west again from Fort Abraham Lincoln under the command of Custer. No one knew precisely where Sitting Bull and his followers were, but the army believed one column or another would find and destroy them.

The Indians are getting bad again. I think we will have some hard times this summer. The old chief Sitting Bull says that he will not make peace.

— *T. P. Eagan, Seventh Cavalry*

On June 6, some three thousand Lakotas and northern Cheyenne camped along Rosebud Creek in southern Montana. There they held their most sacred ceremony, the sun dance. Warriors fasted and danced for days. Sitting Bull slashed his arm one hundred times as a sign of sacrifice, then had a new vision. In it, soldiers attacked his people again, but this time they were upside down, with their horses' hooves in the air and their hats falling to the ground—another omen of victory. The Indians moved their encampment north and were joined by more Indians. Their combined village now had more than six thousand people—nearly two thousand of them warriors—camped along a winding stream they called the Greasy Grass. Whites called it the Little Bighorn.

Custer drove his men relentlessly to find Sitting Bull—twelve miles one day, thirty-three the next, and twenty-eight the next, all under a broiling prairie sun. With him were Arikara and Crow Indian scouts, from tribes the Lakotas had warred against for years and pushed from their traditional hunting grounds. On the cloudless and hot morning of June 25, they spotted Sitting Bull's village from a distant hilltop.

*Members of Custer's
Seventh Cavalry at
Fort Abraham Lincoln*

Although he knew nothing of the terrain and could not tell how many Indians awaited him, Custer decided immediately to attack. The same tactic had succeeded for him in the Civil War and against Black Kettle on the Washita eight years earlier. A victory here seemed just as sure.

He hurried his men toward the Little Bighorn and ordered Major Marcus Reno and 140 men to ride ahead into the village, promising he would reinforce them. But Reno's men were quickly outnumbered, pinned down by Indian warriors, and forced to retreat for their lives. And still Custer did not come.

Custer and his Indian scouts

Instead, perhaps believing that the Indians were fleeing, he led 210 men along a ridge, then down toward another part of the village. Lakota, Cheyenne, and Arapaho warriors swarmed out to turn Custer back, too.

The shots quit coming from the soldiers. Warriors who had crept close to them began to call out that all of the white men were dead.

— *Wooden Leg, northern Cheyenne*

"I called to my men, 'This is a good day to die, follow me,'" a Lakota named Low Dog remembered. "That no man should fall back, every man whipped another man's horse and we rushed right upon them. . . . The soldiers dismounted to fire, but they did very poor shooting. They held their horses' reins on one arm while they were shooting, but their horses were so frightened that they pulled the men all around and a great many of their shots went up into the air and did us no harm."

The fighting, one warrior recalled, lasted no longer than it takes for a hungry man to eat his lunch. Almost one third of Major Reno's command was killed before fresh troops arrived to relieve it. And every man in Custer's group lay dead.

It was the greatest Indian victory of the plains wars.

Kate Bighead, a Cheyenne woman who had survived Custer's attack at Washita eight years earlier, was also at the Little Bighorn. According to her, while Indians were mutilating the dead bodies of the soldiers (so they couldn't fight in the next world), two Cheyenne women found Custer's body and pushed the point of a sewing needle into each of his ears. She explained: "This was done to improve his hearing, as it seemed he had not heard what our chiefs in the South had said when he smoked the pipe with them. They told him then that if ever afterward he should break that peace promise and should fight the Cheyennes, the Everywhere Spirit surely would cause him to be killed."

Americans were celebrating their centennial that summer, proud of one hundred years of independence. The news that George Armstrong Custer and 263 men had been killed by Indians was greeted with simple disbelief. How could people with names that sounded so strange to easterners—Low Dog, Gall, Crazy Horse, Sitting Bull—have defeated so celebrated a soldier?

Sitting Bull had been too weakened from the sun dance to actually fight in the battle. But he was now considered the Indian who had beaten and humiliated the army. Some were even convinced that he couldn't really be an Indian at all or that he was an Indian graduate of West Point, the "red Napoleon."

General Sheridan promised that Custer would be avenged. More troops rushed west, pursuing the defiant Indian bands through the fall

MASSACRED

GEN. CUSTER AND 261 MEN THE VICTIMS.

NO OFFICER OR MAN OF 5 COMPANIES LEFT TO TELL THE TALE.

3 Days Desperate Fighting by Maj. Reno and the Remainder of the Seventh.

Full Details of the Battle.

LIST OF KILLED AND WOUNDED.

THE BISMARCK TRIBUNE'S SPECIAL CORRESPONDENT SLAIN.

Squaws Mutilate and Rob the Dead

Victims Captured Alive Tortured in a Most Fiendish Manner.

What Will Congress Do About It?

Shall This Be the Beginning of the

News of Custer's defeat stunned the nation.

and winter. One by one, they were forced to surrender. Congress ignored the Fort Laramie Treaty of 1868 and took the Black Hills and another forty million acres away from the Lakotas.

We did not give our country to you; you stole it. You come here and tell lies. When you go home, take them with you.

— *Sitting Bull*

But still Sitting Bull did not surrender. With a group of followers, he crossed the border into Canada, beyond the reach of American troops. When an emissary traveled north to offer him a pardon if he would settle on a reservation, Sitting Bull angrily refused. "We did not give our country to you; you stole it," he said. "You come here to tell lies. When you go home, take them with you."

Chief Joseph

Unlike the Lakotas, the Nez Percé tribe of the Northwest had always remained at peace with the United States. They had promised the first whites they had met—the American explorers Lewis and Clark—never to make war on white men. And for three quarters of a century the Nez Percés had kept that promise.

By 1877, most Nez Percés were living on a reservation along the Clearwater River in Idaho. Many had converted to Christianity, wore white man's clothes, and had taken up farming. But some, including a band that lived in the beautiful Wallowa Valley of eastern Oregon, refused to move onto the reservation.

Their village chief, responsible for the overall welfare of his people, was a tall, reserved, but eloquent man named Hin-mah-too-yah-lat-kekht, or Thunder Rolling from the Mountains. Whites called him Chief Joseph.

Six years earlier, Joseph had been called to his father's deathbed. Their homeland was being overwhelmed by white settlers, who claimed that a government treaty permitted it. But Joseph's band had never signed that treaty and insisted that the land still rightfully belonged to them.

"My son," said Joseph's father, "you must stop your ears whenever you are asked to sign a treaty selling your home. Never forget my dying words. This country holds your father's body. Never sell the bones of your father and mother." Joseph had followed his father's wishes yet also managed to stay at peace with the whites crowding into the Wallowa Valley.

But now the government wanted the treaty enforced, regardless of its legitimacy.

Looking Glass, another Nez Percé chief

When Joseph refused once more to sell his homeland, his band and other "non-treaty" Nez Percés were told that if they did not move to the reservation in Idaho, soldiers would be sent to force them.

"I knew I had never sold my country, but I did not want bloodshed," Joseph said. "I did not want my people killed. I did not want *anybody* killed. I said in my heart that, rather than have war, I would give up my country. I would give up my father's grave. I would give up everything rather than have the blood of white men upon the hands of my people."

It has always been the pride of the Nez Percés that they were the friends of the white men. —Chief Joseph

To avoid war, Joseph and the other chiefs reluctantly began moving their people. But a handful of young warriors, seeking revenge for the way the Nez Percés had been treated, slipped away and murdered some white settlers. Joseph realized what the killings meant: Soldiers would be coming. For the first time in their history, whether they intended it or not, the Nez Percés and the United States would be at war.

Nez Percé warriors

It became one of the most remarkable military campaigns in American history. For three and a half months, three different armies with more than two thousand troops and Indian scouts pursued seven hundred Nez Percés as they sought to find friends and a place to rest in peace. Some five hundred of them were women, children, and old people, traveling with their horse herds and belongings, yet they continually outpaced the soldiers over steep, forested mountains and through rugged valleys and sweeping plains.

On several occasions, fresh troops surprised the exhausted Nez Percés and inflicted heavy casualties, but each time the warriors drove soldiers back to provide time for the survivors to escape. "I have been in lots of scrapes," one army veteran remembered of the campaign, "but I never went up against anything like the Nez Percés in all my life."

Finally, after traveling fifteen hundred miles and fighting in seventeen separate battles, Joseph and his people reached the Bear Paw Mountains in northern Montana in late September of 1877. They were only forty miles away from Canada, where they hoped to join Sitting Bull in exile.

But they were surprised one more time. Colonel Nelson A. Miles, leading Custer's old command, had pushed the Seventh Cavalry all the way from eastern Montana to intercept them. With him rode Lakota and Cheyenne warriors, who just a year before had defeated the Seventh at the Little Bighorn but who now had enlisted to help the army fight their longtime enemies, the Nez Percés.

The attack turned into a siege. Many were killed on both sides. The weather turned bitterly cold. Joseph had been just one of many chiefs making decisions during the flight, and his role had been to watch over the safety of the women and children rather than lead the fighting. But now, most of the other chiefs were dead. His people were cold, hungry,

Chief Joseph and his family

and dying from wounds and exhaustion. Miles opened negotiations under a white flag and promised Joseph that if they turned over their rifles, the Nez Percés would be allowed to return home.

On the afternoon of October 5, 1877, Joseph rode out to the foot of a bluff on the prairie. He dismounted from his horse, walked over to the army officers, handed over his gun, and spoke through an interpreter: "I am tired of fighting. Our chiefs are killed. The old men are all dead. It is cold and we have no blankets. The little children are freezing to death. My people, some of them, have run away to the hills, and have no blankets, no food. No one knows where they are — perhaps freezing to death. I want to have time to look for my children, and see how many of them I can find. Maybe I shall find them among the dead. Hear me, my chiefs! I am tired. My heart is sick and sad. From where the sun now stands I will fight no more forever."

Despite the promises—and the efforts of Colonel Miles and other army officers to keep them—Joseph and his people were not returned home.

Instead, the government sent them into exile in Oklahoma's Indian Territory. It was hot and humid there, the opposite of their Wallowa Valley. Many died from malaria and other diseases. They called the place Eeikish Pah, which meant both "the hot place" and "hell."

I am tired of talk that comes to nothing. It makes my heart sick when I remember all the good words and broken promises.
                                                   —Chief Joseph

Joseph took every opportunity he could to meet with government officials, pleading for justice, explaining his people's case, and asking that they be allowed to go home. He traveled several times to Washington, met with two presidents, and gave speeches to large audiences calling for Indians and whites to be treated the same. People liked and admired him and applauded his speeches. But he and his people were kept in "the hot place."

"Good words," Joseph said of the praise he received, "do not last long until they amount to something. Good words do not pay for my dead people.... Good words will not get my people a home where they can live in peace and take care of themselves. I am tired of talk that comes to nothing. It makes my heart sick when I remember all the good words and broken promises."

The Geography of Hope
1877-1887

With the defeat of the Lakotas and Nez Percés, the Indian wars were drawing to a close. The nation prepared to assert control over the entire West.

Between 1877 and 1887, four and a half million more people moved west to inhabit what was called "the geography of hope." Some came seeking freedom, land of their own, and opportunities they couldn't find in the East. Some thought a cattle bonanza on the open plains would never end. Some even believed that their mere presence could alter the West's harsh and unforgiving climate.

As more and more Americans arrived, however, there seemed to be less and less room for anyone who seemed different in any way. Native Americans—especially the children—were expected to give up their culture. Spanish-speaking westerners found themselves outnumbered and overwhelmed by the newcomers, even in towns they had lived in for centuries.

And the Chinese, who had done more than almost anyone to connect the West to the rest of the nation, would be told they were no longer welcome.

But even as Americans tried to "tame" the West and make its people conform, they preferred the colorful and romantic version of it presented by Buffalo Bill Cody, the nation's greatest showman. Half frontiersman, half fraud, he gave them a "Wild West"—full of adventure, myth, and violence, all of which they could enjoy from the safety of their bleacher seats.

•◦• •◦• •◦•

Benjamin "Pap" Singleton and one of his promotional leaflets

In 1877, federal troops that had occupied the South since the end of the Civil War were withdrawn, and new state laws began to restrict the rights of freed slaves. Many African Americans were forced into sharecropping—renting land in exchange for a percentage of the crops they grew. In practice, however, the sharecroppers fell once again under the power of their former masters.

"It's no use," sharecropper John Solomon Lewis told his landlord. "I works hard and raises big crops and you sells it and keeps the money and brings me more and more in debt. So I will go somewhere else and try to make headway like white working-men." All over the South, committees of African Americans formed to seek some means of escape. Some favored emigrating to Africa or moving north to Canada.

But Benjamin "Pap" Singleton, an ex-slave from Tennessee, believed that the open spaces of the West offered more hope. He persuaded three hundred former slaves to move to eastern Kansas, where they settled a place called the Singleton Colony. Then he began distributing leaflets urging more African Americans to "come and join us in the promised land."

Soon, tens of thousands were on their way, willing to risk everything they had for the chance of a new life. Some took riverboats up the Missouri River. Others, too poor to pay their passage, walked all the way from Mississippi, Louisiana, and Kentucky. They called themselves Exodusters, from the story in the Bible about the migration of the Hebrews out of bondage in Egypt.

John Solomon Lewis was one of them. When he crossed into Kansas, he remembered, "I looked on the ground and I says this is free ground. Then I looked on the heavens and I says them is free and beautiful heavens. Then I looked within my heart and I says to myself I wonder why I was never free before? I asked my wife, did she know the ground she stands on. She said, 'No.' I said it is free ground and she cried for joy."

When I landed on the soil of Kansas, I looked on the ground and I says this is free ground.

—John Solomon Lewis

African Americans weren't the only ones moving west. Railroads and state governments were eager to sell land on the western Great Plains. Because of its lack of rainfall, the

An Exoduster family and their new home in Kansas

region had been called "the Great American Desert" and passed over by earlier homesteaders. As it happened, the 1870s and early 1880s were unusually wet years in the West, and the prairies were yielding bumper crops. But the land promoters promised that something more permanent had occurred. The influx of settlers, they said, had somehow changed the climate for good.

"Rain follows the plow" was the phrase they used. Many believed it. Within ten years, the populations of Colorado and Nebraska doubled. The populations of South Dakota, Montana, and Wyoming tripled.

Cattlemen rushed in, too. The federally owned grasslands seemed limitless—and so did the profits of men who turned huge herds loose on them for free. Wealthy men from England, Scotland, Europe, and the eastern states invested their money in what was advertised as the great "beef bonanza."

But then a series of harsh winters, especially the winter of 1886 to 1887, killed hundreds of thousands of helpless cattle on the Great Plains. "A

Moving cattle in a blizzard

business that had been fascinating to me before suddenly became distasteful," said one rancher after viewing the carcasses that littered the prairies. "I never wanted to own again an animal that I could not feed and shelter." The days on the open range were coming to an end.

I saw countless carcasses of cattle going down with the ice, rolling over and over as they went.... For days on end, tearing down with the grinding ice cakes, went Death's cattle roundup.

—Lincoln Lang, rancher

The ranchers had learned they could not ignore the West's climate. And the homesteaders soon learned that they had not changed it.

The wet years came to an end. Some places on the high plains emptied just as quickly as they had filled, as drought and hard times drove settlers off their farms. But some homesteaders—Exodusters and whites alike—stuck it out. In the West, they realized, hope and opportunity often existed side by side with disappointment and hardship. "Free" ground was not necessarily "easy" ground.

Virtually all Indian tribes had been confined to reservations by 1883. Even Sitting Bull and his small band of Lakotas, who had struggled to survive in Canada after defeating Custer, had surrendered and been sent to the Standing Rock reservation in North Dakota. For every Indian, there were now forty whites in the West.

Apache children, upon arrival at the Carlisle Indian School...

and four months later

Like Indians on all the other reservations, the Lakotas were expected to give up their own language and speak English, to abandon their traditional religious customs, and to live in log cabins and learn to farm. Every two weeks, some scrawny steers were brought in, and men who only a few years earlier had hunted buffalo on the open plains now shot fenced-in cattle for food.

But the quickest way to "Americanize" Native Americans, some people believed, was to concentrate on their children. "I believe in immersing the Indian in our civilization," said Richard Henry Pratt, "and when we get them under, holding them there until they are thoroughly soaked." Pratt was part of a group of people who called

themselves the Friends of the Indian, and he founded the United States Indian Training and Industrial School at Carlisle, Pennsylvania.

Indian boys and girls as young as five were taken from their families and sent halfway across the continent to the school. Often, their parents' permission was not even asked. Mothers, fearing for the children's safety and worried they would never see their sons or daughters again, sometimes sent along special "medicine bundles" for the child to ward off evil spirits.

Our belongings were taken from us, even the little medicine bags our mothers had given us to protect us from harm. Everything was placed in a heap and set afire.

— *Lone Wolf*

At the school, the children's hair was cut—even though for some tribes, long hair was a sign of pride and strength—and they were given names like Philip Sheridan and Ulysses S. Grant to replace their real names. "Our belongings were taken from us, even the little medicine bags our mothers had given us to protect us from harm," remembered Lone Wolf, a Blackfoot. "Everything was placed in a heap and set afire."

They were given military uniforms, marched into classes where they were taught English and industrial skills, and forbidden to speak their

Native American students at a reservation school in Arizona

native languages. Mary Armstrong remembered being caught speaking Cheyenne one day and having her mouth washed out with a lye soap that was so harsh it blistered her tongue.

Within twenty years, there were twenty-four other off-reservation schools like Carlisle, as well as eighty-one boarding schools and 147 day schools on the reservations. Each of them required separating Indian children from their parents, and each sought to achieve the same goal. "Education," said one Friend of the Indian, "should seek the disintegration of the tribes. They should be educated, not as Indians, but as Americans."

The push to make the West and its people more like the rest of the nation extended beyond Indians and the reservations.

Bob Tail, a Cheyenne, and his "Americanized" son

In Utah, the Mormons had worked for half a century to carve out their own unique society. The church owned many of the territory's biggest businesses, had its own political party, often carried out its own laws and punishments in defiance of federal judges, and encouraged the practice of polygamy, in which some men had more than one wife.

During the 1880s, Congress cracked down on the Mormons. Polygamists were thrown in jail. Plural wives and their children were separated from their husbands. Laws were passed threatening to confiscate church property. Finally, in order to save their religion, church leaders abandoned some of Mormonism's most distinctive features. The church's political party was disbanded, its businesses were sold, and polygamy was renounced. Utah—which had been founded as a sanctuary from the United States—was admitted to the Union as the forty-fifth state.

Most of the three hundred thousand Chinese in the United States were also in the West. They had helped build the transcontinental railroad that made development of the West possible. Now they could be found digging

An anti-Chinese cartoon depicts San Francisco being overrun by immigrants.

irrigation ditches and planting vineyards in California, operating laundries and restaurants, working in western factories, and running fishing fleets up and down the coast.

But when an economic depression struck in the 1870s, out-of-work westerners began to blame the Chinese. "We intend to try and vote the Chinaman out, to frighten him out, and if this won't do, to kill him out," said Denis Kearney, head of the California Workingmen's Party.

Anti-Chinese riots erupted throughout the West. In Rock Springs, Wyoming, twenty-eight Chinese were murdered. In Tacoma, Washington, state militiamen had to be called out to restore order. The Chinese in Seattle were rounded up, pushed onto boats, and forced out to sea.

An ambitious and well-educated Chinese man named Chung Sun had arrived in California carrying six hundred dollars and dreaming of starting a tea plantation. But he almost immediately found himself caught up in an anti-Chinese riot in Los Angeles, in which he was beaten and robbed of his savings.

Chung Sun didn't give up. He made his way north to the town of Watsonville and found a job digging ditches. "Being a man of education and culture, I am capable of other work," he wrote. "But my philosophy teaches me [that] any useful work is more honorable than idleness. I shall therefore, with patience, continue to dig with an abiding hope for something better."

We intend to try and vote the Chinaman out, to frighten him out, and if this won't do, to kill him out.

— Denis Kearney, California Workingmen's Party

When the ditch was finished, however, Chung Sun couldn't find another job. No one would hire him. California's legislature had passed laws making it illegal to employ Chinese workers. He moved on to San

Francisco and set sail for home. "I hope you will pardon my expressing a painful disappointment," he wrote, "but such prejudice can only prevail among the ignorant."

I hope you will pardon my expressing a painful disappointment, but such prejudice can only prevail among the ignorant.
— Chung Sun

In 1882, western politicians and labor unions persuaded Congress to pass the Chinese Exclusion Act. The year before it passed, nearly forty thousand Chinese entered the United States. The next year, just twenty-three were allowed in.

Los Angeles in the 1870s seemed much as it had thirty years earlier, when the United States had taken California from Mexico. It was still a largely Hispanic farming town with a population of fewer than ten thousand people. San Francisco, with nearly 150,000 people, was still the largest city in California—and the West.

Then, in the mid-1880s, two railroads built lines into Los Angeles and immediately began a fare war. A passenger could ride all the way from St. Louis for as little as one dollar. Promoters advertised southern California as a Garden of Eden. "The air, when inhaled, gives to the individual a stimulus and vital force," one booster boasted. A doctor claimed that moving to Los Angeles would add at least ten extra years to a person's life.

Los Angeles in the early 1870s

Easterners began arriving in larger and larger numbers—120,000 in 1887 alone. Midwestern farmers moved onto what had been the ranches of native Californios and began planting lemons, grapefruits, and oranges.

Real estate promoters poured in, too—so many that the hotels ran out of beds and rented them bathtubs to sleep in. They staged

Los Angeles in the late 1880s

picnics, barbecues, and circuses to pull in customers, sometimes offering house lots in communities that didn't even exist. But in two and a half years, sixty new towns were founded in Los Angeles County.

One of them was started by a religious man from Ohio who established what he hoped would be a model community. Free land was offered to any congregation willing to put up a church. Liquor, gambling, and other vices were to be permanently prohibited. His wife named the new town for a friend's country home back in Ohio—Hollywood.

Within ten years, Los Angeles and its county's population had grown tenfold. And the city's Mexican-American heart—now known as the barrio—had been surrounded.

William F. Cody had done many of the things a young man could do in the West. During the building of the transcontinental railroad, he had hunted buffalo to feed the hungry crews—and earned the nickname that stayed with him all his life: Buffalo Bill. He'd been a horse wrangler, cattle rancher, gold seeker, land speculator, and army scout.

Cody was a genuine westerner, but he also had a natural talent for calling attention to himself. After the Battle of the Little Bighorn, Cody had taken part in the army's campaign to avenge Custer's death and defeat. Buffalo Bill led the cavalry within sight of a small band of Cheyenne warriors. There was a fight. One chief was killed. Cody took the chief's scalp and mailed it to his own sister, who fainted when she opened the parcel. Soon, with great embellishment, he was reenacting "The First Scalp for Custer" in theaters all over the East.

William F. Cody: Buffalo Bill

Buffalo Bill, said cowboy Teddy Blue Abbott, "was the only one that had brains enough to make that Wild West stuff pay money. I remember one time he came into a saloon in North Platte, and he took off his hat and that long hair of his that he had rolled up under his hat fell down on his shoulders. It always bothered him, so he rolled it back under his hat again and Brady the saloon man says: 'Say, Bill, why the hell don't you cut the damn stuff off?' And Cody says: 'If I did, I'd starve to death.'"

In 1883, Cody moved from the stage and launched a larger extravaganza called "Buffalo Bill's Wild West — America's National Entertainment." For the next thirty years, twice a day, six days a week, he presented his colorful version of the West to the world. He toured from Chicago to Philadelphia, Paris to Munich. On Staten Island one summer, a million people attended the shows; another million paid to see him that winter at Madison Square Garden in New York. "Each scene is instructive," one advertisement promised. "A year's visit West in three hours."

*B*uffalo Bill was the only one that had brains enough to make that Wild West stuff pay money.

— Teddy Blue Abbott

There were Pony Express riders, Mexican vaqueros displaying their skills with the lasso, a buffalo hunt, and much more. A wagon train was raided by Indians — and saved by Buffalo Bill. A settler's cabin was attacked — and saved by Buffalo Bill. The authentic Deadwood Stagecoach was surrounded by Indians — and saved by Buffalo Bill.

*Buffalo Bill's Wild West
show toured the world.*

But the grand finale was a reenactment of the Battle of the Little Bighorn, "showing with historical accuracy," the handbills claimed, "the scene of Custer's last stand." And at the end, there was Buffalo Bill himself, in the center of the battlefield with his hat off—while behind him the words "TOO LATE" were projected onto a screen.

Crowds couldn't get enough of it. Even Elizabeth Custer, who had been widowed by the actual event, proclaimed it "the most realistic and faithful representation of a western life that has ceased to be." She came back to see it many times.

For millions of people all over the world, Buffalo Bill's Wild West show and the actual history of the West's settlement had become the same thing.

Each scene is instructive. A year's visit West in three hours.

— *Buffalo Bill advertisement*

Like Cody himself, there were others in the show who blurred the line between an authentic western reality and a mythic West. There was Buck Taylor, the "King of the Cowboys"; Con Groner, "Cowboy Sheriff of the Platte," who claimed to have captured more than fifty murderers; and Miss Phoebe Anne Moses, "The

Little Sure Shot" from Ohio, who looked into a mirror and shot backward over her shoulder to break small glass balls and who was better known under her stage name, Annie Oakley. Hundreds of Lakota warriors also worked in Buffalo Bill's show, seeing in it a chance to earn money and escape the reservation.

In 1885, the most famous Indian in America joined the entourage—Sitting Bull, billed as "the slayer of General Custer." He was paid fifty dollars a week, a bonus of $125, and reserved the right to profit directly from the sale of autographs and pictures of himself. Sitting Bull was wildly popular with audiences, although some of Custer's admirers booed him from the stands when he rode around the arena once a show. Afterward, awestruck visitors came to peer at him in his tepee and asked him to sign his name for them.

Sitting Bull liked Cody. The showman gave him a handsome hat and the gray horse he'd ridden in the arena as gifts. But Sitting Bull could not understand why beggars were left to drift about the streets of big cities, and he gave much of his pay away to news-boys and hoboes he met on the tour.

Two of the show's biggest stars: Annie Oakley and Sitting Bull

After four months with the Wild West show, he returned to his home at the Standing Rock reservation. There, he had another of his mystical visions about the future.

In 1876, one vision had warned him that white men were pursuing the Lakotas. Another had predicted that Custer's soldiers at the Little Bighorn would fall into the village, upside down.

But now Sitting Bull had a new vision. This one was equally clear. Wandering alone near his home one morning, he watched a meadowlark flutter down onto a small hill. Then the bird spoke to him, saying, "Your own people, *Lakotas*, will kill you."

One Sky Above Us
1887 into the Twentieth Century

*The World's
Columbian Exposition*

The four hundredth anniversary of Christopher Columbus's arrival in the New World was celebrated in Chicago in 1893—a year late. The World's Columbian Exposition was so large and so ambitious that it took an extra year just to get everything ready.

It was an extravaganza. The first Ferris wheel was unveiled. California's pavilion displayed a huge statue of a conquistador, made entirely of prunes. Kansas showed off a big herd of buffalo—*stuffed*. And Buffalo Bill Cody's Wild West show delighted audiences with his colorful version of a frontier that seemed to have closed.

There were sixty-three million Americans in 1893. Some twenty-four million people paid their way into the fair, more than had attended any other event in the history of the world.

The Americans' pride and enthusiasm was understandable. In less than fifty years, the United States had stretched its boundaries to the Pacific Ocean and altered everything in its path. The conquest of the West that had begun with Coronado at last seemed complete.

But beyond the fairgrounds, beyond Chicago, in the real West, for every frontier story that was coming to an end, another one was beginning.

•◆• •◆• •◆•

On the morning of April 22, 1889, some one hundred thousand eager settlers surrounded what was called the Oklahoma District on the southern plains. Nearly two million acres in the heart of Indian Territory were

A family waits for the start of the Oklahoma land rush.

being opened for homesteading. All along the district's borders, people were poised for the land rush to begin.

At precisely noon, bugles blew and the huge crowd surged forward. Some rode horses. Some pedaled bicycles. Others climbed aboard special trains and leapt off at the locations of towns about to be born: Oklahoma City, Stillwater, Kingfisher, Norman, and the site of the proposed territorial capital, Guthrie.

Men fell over each other in heaps, others stumbled and fell headlong, while many ran forward so blindly that...they passed the best of the town lots.

—HARPER'S WEEKLY

"Men jumped from the roofs of the moving cars at the risk of their lives," wrote one reporter at Guthrie. "Some were so stunned by the fall that they could not get up for some minutes. Men fell over each other in heaps, others stumbled and fell headlong, while many ran forward so blindly that . . . they passed the best of the town lots."

A wild scramble began to stake claims on parcels of land, but the most valuable locations had already been taken by settlers who had illegally slipped through the night before. They called themselves Sooners.

By nightfall, all 1,920,000 acres of the Oklahoma District had been claimed. And Guthrie was a tent city with fifteen thousand residents.

The following day, the new citizens began choosing Guthrie's mayor. It wasn't easy. There were no ballots, so two lines formed, one for each

The stampede for land begins.

candidate. But so many voters ran to the back of the line to vote for their choice a second time that the election had to be done over.

Three men without a cent between them opened a bank. Deposits were kept in a pot-bellied stove until they could afford a vault. An elderly woman named Button Mary opened for business, reattaching buttons on bachelors' shirts for ten cents each. A blacksmith realized that

Two of Guthrie's first citizens guard their claim.

Guthrie needed a dentist, so he simply declared himself one. To advertise his skills, he hung teeth he had pulled out on a string outside his tent.

Within five days, wood-frame buildings were being banged together on Main Street. And by the time Guthrie was one month old, it had a hotel, three newspapers, three general stores, and fifty saloons.

There would be more land rushes and more waves of homesteaders all across the West, bringing in settlers and creating new towns in numbers never before imagined. By the end of the 1880s, nearly 17 million people lived west of the Mississippi River. By 1920, that number would increase to 31 million.

Most of the newcomers would live not in the wide open spaces but in cities. The West was becoming more urban, more industrial, more like the East.

The citizens of Butte, Montana, boasted they lived on the "richest hill on earth"—an underground deposit that yielded more than a million dollars every month in copper, the metal that made the electrical age possible. As with the gold rush of 1849, Butte's mines attracted people from all over the globe, except now they came as industrial workers instead of independent prospectors. Deep in its mine shafts, where "No Smoking" signs

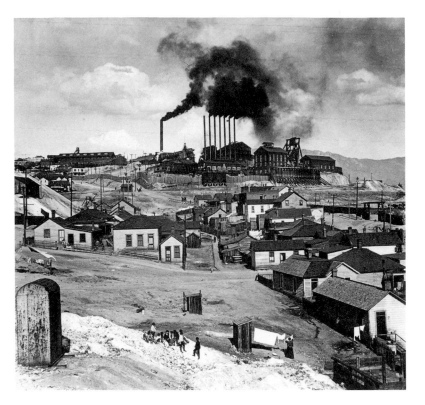

Butte, Montana:
"the richest hill on earth"

were posted in fourteen different languages, men labored in dangerous, unsanitary conditions. Many of them died young from silicosis, caused by inhaling dust that tore at their lungs.

Above ground, Butte was one of the dirtiest towns in America. Just four trees survived in the city, and all the nearby hillsides had been stripped of wood to fuel the copper smelters that roared on, day and night. Thick smoke hung over Butte, so dense and dark sometimes that streetlights were turned on in the middle of the day. It seemed, one historian said, "a misplaced eastern town, a kind of downsized Pittsburgh located in the middle of the Rocky Mountains."

In Los Angeles, the population quadrupled between 1890 and 1904, to nearly two hundred thousand residents. But if it was to continue growing, it would have to overcome the same restraint that cities had faced dating back four hundred years to the time of the first Indians in the region: not enough water.

Los Angeles found its water 223 miles away, in the Owens River valley of the Sierra Nevada. There, small farmers were using river water to irrigate their apple orchards and hay fields. But through a combination of deception and raw political power, Los Angeles got control of the water rights. Then it built a series of canals, tunnels, and aqueducts to move the precious water through the mountains and across the Mojave Desert. The West had seen nothing like it since the building of the transcontinental railroad.

Owens Valley never recovered from the loss. But with its water, Los Angeles boomed again—and soon surpassed San Francisco as the biggest and most powerful city in the West.

•◆•

As the nineteenth century drew to a close, Native Americans continued to lose their land. Some also began to lose hope.

In 1887, Congress passed a new law, the Dawes General Allotment Act. It provided each Indian family with 160 acres of land and then opened up the remaining acres on a reservation for white settlement. The law was intended to help Indians by turning them into homesteaders. Instead, it devastated them. Within twenty years of its passage, two thirds of the land that had been in Indian hands was gone.

On the reservations, government rations were reduced. Diseases such as whooping cough, tuberculosis, and influenza spread. The crackdown against native languages and native customs intensified.

In 1890, in the midst of the hard times, a new movement swept through many western tribes. It was called the Ghost Dance, and it offered hope to people who desperately needed it. If they performed the Ghost Dance ceremony, some Indians believed, all that had occurred during the last century would disappear as if it had merely been a bad dream. "The dead are to return," one Lakota said of the Ghost Dance's promise. "The buffalo are to return. The Lakota people will get back their own way of life. The white people will soon go away, and that will mean happier times once more. That part about the dead returning was what appealed to me. To think I should see my dear mother, grandmother, brothers, and sisters again!"

Lakotas gather for a Ghost Dance.

As the Ghost Dance spread through the Lakota reservations in South Dakota, the government agent panicked and called for troops. Nelson A. Miles, now a general, was sent with five thousand soldiers, including the Seventh Cavalry.

At the Standing Rock reservation in North Dakota, the Lakota leader Sitting Bull was skeptical at first about the Ghost Dance's promised powers. But he agreed to let his people learn it if they wished. Then, Indian police—charged with keeping peace among their own tribe—reported that the aging medicine man planned to leave his reservation and join the Ghost Dancers farther south. Some forty-three Indian policemen were dispatched to quietly arrest him.

Before dawn on December 15, 1890, the police burst into Sitting Bull's cabin, ordered him to his feet, and pushed him toward the door. Outside, his followers began to gather, shouting at the Lakota police and vowing to stop the arrest of their leader.

My brothers, I bring you word from your fathers the ghosts, that they are marching now to join you.

— Wovoka, Paiute medicine man and Ghost Dance prophet

Sitting Bull hesitated, unsure what to do. One of his supporters raised his rifle and shot one of the policemen. Both sides began firing. Fourteen Lakotas died, including Sitting Bull, who had been shot through the head by a Lakota policeman. The last of Sitting Bull's great visions had come to pass: He had been killed by his own people.

The tragedy did not end there. Sitting Bull's grieving followers joined a band of Lakotas led by Chief Big Foot and headed toward the Pine Ridge reservation in South Dakota, hoping things could be settled peacefully. General Miles misunderstood what they were doing and sent the Seventh Cavalry to intercept them.

Three days after Christmas, the soldiers caught up with Big Foot and the others. The chief, sick with pneumonia, rode in a wagon that displayed a white flag to show his peaceful intentions. An army doctor did what he could for Big Foot, and the soldiers distributed rations to the 120 men and 230 women and children in his band. But the Seventh also posted four small cannons on the top of a rise overlooking the Lakota camp. They all settled down for the night along a creek called Wounded Knee.

The next morning, troops began moving from tepee to tepee, confiscating knives, axes, and rifles from the Indians. Tensions mounted. A medicine man began to dance. "Do not fear," he told the warriors, "but let your hearts be strong. Many soldiers are about us and have many bullets, but I am assured the bullets cannot penetrate us." Ghost Dance shirts, he said, would protect them.

At the same time, soldiers tried to disarm a Lakota who was deaf. He held on to his rifle. There was a struggle, and it went off. Then shots erupted everywhere. The soldiers began firing the cannons as the Lakotas did their best to fight back.

The fighting lasted less than an hour. When the shooting stopped, some 250 Lakotas were dead. Dead, too, were twenty-five soldiers. Wounded Lakotas and soldiers alike were taken to a church at Pine Ridge, where an injured young girl with a Ghost Dance shirt underneath her clothes said to a nurse, "They told me if I put this on, the bullets would not go through, and I believed them. Now see where we are."

The burial pit at Wounded Knee

Fighting sputtered on for several weeks across the reservation, until some four thousand Lakotas surrendered to General Miles. At Wounded Knee, when a government burial party finally arrived, it found the bodies of dead Lakotas still lying where they had fallen. The frozen corpses were loaded into wagons and dumped into a mass grave.

On October 20, 1905, a stagecoach rattled north toward the Sweetwater River in central Wyoming. On board was an unusual passenger, a young woman named Ethel Waxham.

Ethel Waxham...

She was a city girl, a graduate of an eastern college, fluent in four languages—and intensely curious about the world. "I do not want to see one side of life only, but many," she told a friend. Now she was on her way to her first full-time job, as a schoolteacher.

Waxham soon found the new experiences she had been seeking. The school was a one-room building with a sod roof and a door riddled with bullet holes. There were only seven students. The closest lived one mile away. Another rode a horse five miles to attend classes. During the winter, snowstorms delayed the mail for weeks, and temperatures dipped to 45 degrees below zero. "The ink in all seven bottles was frozen as well as the glue, in the morning," she wrote in her diary, "and would have to be thawed out daily before the stove."

Visitors to the ranch where Waxham stayed were rare. But among those who showed up with increasing regularity—despite a difficult eleven-hour ride—was a sheep rancher named John Galloway Love. He had come to Wyoming in 1891, walking the last hundred miles after his

and her one-room school in Wyoming

horses died from drinking bad water. Since then, he had spent years on the range, herding other people's sheep, caring for their cattle, and saving up enough money to start a ranch of his own on a treeless stretch of land along a stream called Muskrat Creek.

Ethel Waxham enjoyed Love's sharp wit and his friendship, but when he proposed marriage, she turned him down and went on with her work. When the school year ended, she left Wyoming and went back to college in Colorado for a master's degree in literature. She took a teaching job in Wisconsin, then came back and spent another year in Colorado.

But everywhere she went, letters from Love pursued her:

John Love

Muskrat, Wyoming
November 12, 1906
Dear Miss Waxham,
...I know that you have not been brought up to cook and labor. I have never been on the lookout for a slave and would not utter a word of [complaint] if you never learned, or if you got ambitious and made a "batch" of biscuits that proved fatal to my favorite dog. I honestly believe that I could idolize you to such an extent as to not utter a harsh word....I will do my level best to win you....If I fail, I will still want your friendship just the same.

We had one very hard storm and several herders lost their lives, but that, I think, was their own fault.

Dear Miss Waxham,
...I for one am glad that your curiosity led you to drift up here to Wyoming, and now my supreme desire is to persuade you to come back....

For five years, though she gave him little encouragement, Love doggedly courted Ethel Waxham by mail. And all the while, he worked to build a ranch he hoped would someday be their home. He scoured the countryside for abandoned buildings and hauled them over rough roads to Muskrat Creek. A saloon and an old hotel were transformed into bunkhouses, sheds, and a blacksmith shop. The main house was built with logs that Love had to cut in the Wind River Mountains, a hundred miles away; each trip took him two weeks.

He tended his growing herds of

Dear Miss Waxham, I will do my level best to win you....If I fail, I will still want your friendship just the same.
—*John Love*

sheep, cattle, and horses. To water the crops he intended to grow, he began work on two dams and a long irrigation ditch, working by hand and by horse.

And he kept writing letters.

October 12th, 1909
Dear Miss Waxham,
...I have been in the saddle all day and am rather tired....I have a nice
coal fire burning in the wagon now as the nights are rather frosty. Your
picture, nicely framed, adorns the wagon....No end of work to do, but still
I am contented.

Yours sincerely,
John G. Love

Finally, in the spring of 1910, Ethel Waxham agreed to be John Love's wife and moved into the home he had prepared on Muskrat Creek. It was seventy miles from the part of Wyoming where she had taught, and it was more remote, more treeless, more immense than she had expected. "The sheer alone-ness of it is unique," she wrote. "Never a light but one's own at night. No smoke from another's fire in sight." In an area the size of Rhode Island, the Loves were the only inhabitants.

Like so many western settlers before them, the Loves began with big dreams—large herds of livestock, abundant orchards and irrigated fields of grain, a better life for their children. And like many before them, they encountered hardships, disappointments, and setbacks. They met each

Ranch life was full
of hard work.

one with grit, determination, and unshakable hope for the future.

A severe winter killed most of their sheep. Fash floods destroyed the irrigation dams. Bankers foreclosed on Love's loans, taking what livestock he had left. "What will you do with the baby?" a banker asked Ethel Love as she watched the foreclosure with her first-born in her arms. She answered, "I think I'll keep him."

At age forty-three, all of Love's work had ended in ruin. But he still had his land and his family, which soon included three children. He hired himself out as a common sheepherder for forty dollar a month—and started over yet again.

The Loves and two of their children

Ethel became her children's teacher. Their schoolhouse was their home, without electricity or running water but filled with books, which they read by kerosene light. Their lesson desk was an old gambling table their father had salvaged from a ghost town.

As the years passed, there were more setbacks. Fire destroyed one of the ranch buildings. A Wyoming oil boom passed them by. One year, shipping cattle to Omaha ended up costing Love twenty-seven dollars more than he received for them in sale. Disease took another sheep herd. A bank failed, and with it went the family savings.

But John and Ethel Love never gave up. Despite the hardships the West threw at them, they struggled forward on Muskrat Creek. They watched their children grow, go off to college, and succeed in life. One of their children, David, believed that his parents were typical of many of the people who settled the West. During the winter of 1919, influenza had nearly crippled him and his father, and they had to help each other learn to walk again. He said: "I can still remember us standing together, each leaning on the other,

We live the ranchiest kind of ranch life.... The sheer alone-ness of it is unique — never a light but one's own at night. No smoke from another's fire in sight.

— Ethel Waxham Love

this six-year-old boy and the fifty-year-old man, and his saying, 'Well, laddy, even we can make it.' So, of course, we did."

Twenty-five years after fighting his reluctant war with the United States, Chief Joseph of the Nez Percés still longed to return home.

He and his people had finally been allowed to leave Oklahoma but were now confined to a reservation in eastern Washington, far from their beloved homeland in Oregon's Wallowa Valley.

Chief Joseph in later years

Before he died, in 1904, Joseph continued to take every possible opportunity to speak out on behalf of his people—and all Native Americans. "Whenever the white man treats the Indian as they treat each other, then we will have no more wars," he said. "We shall all be alike—brothers of one father, and one mother, with one sky above us and one country around us, and one government for all. Then the Great Spirit who rules above will smile upon this land, and send rain to wash out the bloody spots made by brothers' hands from the face of the earth."

At the time, fewer than 250,000 Native Americans were left in the country—the fewest the continent had ever held. Some people now referred to Indians as the "vanishing race."

But Native Americans weren't vanishing. They were persevering, adapting, surviving. And they were following different paths to do it.

No one demonstrated this more clearly than Buffalo Bird Woman and her brother Wolf Chief, Hidatsa Indians from North Dakota. During

*W*henever the white man treats the Indian as they treat each other, then we will have no more wars. We shall all be alike — brothers of one father, and one mother, with one sky above us and one country around us, and one government for all. — Chief Joseph

their long lifetimes, they witnessed astounding changes. The buffalo was replaced by the cow. The horse was replaced by the automobile. And the earth lodge villages of the Hidatsas, once the most populous towns on the northern plains, gave way to growing towns and cities of white settlers.

Buffalo Bird Woman responded by holding fast to her traditional beliefs. She spoke only her native language and practiced traditional customs, including singing songs to the corn crops she tended in the ways of her ancestors. And before she died, in the 1920s, she explained her people's traditions to someone who would write them all down. That way, she hoped, they would never be forgotten.

Wolf Chief and
Buffalo Bird Woman

Wolf Chief, however, followed a different path for survival. He learned English, converted to Christianity, opened his own store on the reservation, and over the course of forty years wrote more than a hundred letters to Washington, D.C., trying to help his people. Whenever other Hidatsas scorned him as "trying to be a white man," Wolf Chief had an answer. "I want to be strong," he said, "and go forward."

Regardless of the path they followed, Native Americans did go forward. Not only did they not "vanish"; they grew. By 1990, there were nearly two million Native Americans in the United States. They can be found today in all parts of the West — from the Zuñis of New Mexico, who were the first to encounter Coronado, to the Gabrielinos of southern California, on whose land the West's biggest city, Los Angeles, now stands; from the Nez Percés of Idaho, who sheltered Lewis and Clark and made a solemn promise of peace with the United States, to the Lakotas of South Dakota, who fought the United States over the Black Hills and are struggling still for their return. They can be found in every walk of life and in every profession, going forward and yet also keeping their traditions alive.

•◆•

Other westerners moved forward, too, often in the same traditions and patterns that have marked the West's history. In the twentieth century, newcomers have arrived from every direction. Japanese, Filipinos, and Koreans reached the region by going east—as did the Chinese, once the Exclusion Act was repealed. Fresh arrivals poured in from every European nation. And over the first quarter of this century, 1.5 million men, women, and children—10 percent of the population of Mexico—left their country and came north, hoping for a better life and following the same routes once taken by the conquistadors.

Even today, the West is the fastest growing section of the nation, a magnet to foreign immigrants and Americans alike. They come pursuing different dreams, as newcomers to the West always have. Those dreams often collide with other people's dreams. And although not every dream comes true, each one is pursued by individuals who believe, as John Love did, that "even we can make it" in the West.

From the beginnings of time, the West has been a land of myth. "It is a dream landscape," according to N. Scott Momaday, a Pulitzer Prize–winning writer and a Kiowa. "It's a landscape that has to be seen to be believed. And it may have to be *believed* in order to be seen." It has been the land of the Seven Cities of Gold and the Northwest Passage. It has been Gum San, the "gold mountain," and it has been the place where "rain follows the plow."

The land itself is as awe-inspiring and majestic today as it ever was. And it is still a mythic place, a "dream landscape." Millions of tourists travel each year to peer into the Grand Canyon that once amazed Coronado's men, to marvel at the geysers that once surprised mountain man Joe Meek, or to hike in the mountains that forty-niner William Swain found so difficult to cross. Millions more—whether or not they ever travel west—flock to movies set in the West, watch commercials that use western landscapes as a backdrop, even buy their clothes at "western wear" stores.

Just as the historical story of the West never ends, neither does its grip on people's imagination. No one knows for sure why one place is filled with so much myth and so many dreams. But no one disputes that the West is such a place.

"The western landscape carries an enormous emotional weight, not only with Americans, but with much of the world," writer and historian Tom Watkins says. "There's always been a place in human history that became the depository of all the dreams, hopes, and aspirations of people — someplace that was always going to be better than where they are. The West still has that characteristic. It is probably the one single thing that makes it unique in American history: that a place so wide and large and various could at the same time be a single repository of so much hope."

Principal Sources

General

Billington, Ray Allen, and Martin Ridge. *Westward Expansion*. New York: Macmillan, 1982.

White, Richard. *It's Your Misfortune and None of My Own: A History of the American West*. Norman: University of Oklahoma Press, 1991.

The People

Ballantine, Betty, and Ian Ballantine, editors. *The Native Americans: An Illustrated History*. Atlanta: Turner, 1993.

Duncan, Dayton. *Out West: American Journey Along the Lewis and Clark Trail*. New York: Penguin, 1987.

Grinnell, George Bird. *The Cheyenne Indians*. New Haven: Yale University Press, 1923; Lincoln: University of Nebraska Press, 1972.

Moulton, Gary E., editor. *The Journals of the Lewis and Clark Expedition*. Lincoln: University of Nebraska Press, 1986.

Ronda, James P. *Lewis and Clark Among the Indians*. Lincoln: University of Nebraska Press, 1984.

Stands in Timber, John, and Margot Liberty. *Cheyenne Memories*. New Haven: Yale University Press, 1967.

Weber, David J. *The Spanish Frontier in North America*. New Haven: Yale University Press, 1992.

Empire Upon the Trails

DeVoto, Bernard. *The Year of Decision: 1846.* Boston: Houghton Mifflin, 1942.

Thompson, Erwin N. *Shallow Grave at Waiilatpu: The Sagers' West.* Portland, Oregon: Oregon Historical Society Press, Western Imprints, 1985.

Vestal, Stanley. *Joe Meek: The Merry Mountain Man.* Lincoln: University of Nebraska Press, 1952.

Weber, David J. *The Mexican Frontier, 1821–1846.* Albuquerque: University of New Mexico Press, 1982.

———, editor. *Foreigners in Their Native Land.* Albuquerque: University of New Mexico Press, 1973.

Weems, John Edward. *Dreams of Empire.* New York: Simon and Schuster, 1971.

The Speck of the Future

Beilharz, Edwin A., and Carlos U. Lopez, translators and editors. *We Were 49ers! Chilean Accounts of the California Gold Rush.* Pasadena, Calif.: Ward Ritchie Press, 1976.

Dillinger, William C. *The Gold Discovery: James Marshall and the California Gold Rush.* Sacramento: California Department of Parks and Recreation, 1990.

Holliday, J. S. *The World Rushed In: An Eyewitness Account of a Nation Heading West.* New York: Simon and Schuster, 1981.

Rawls, James J. *Indians of California: The Changing Image.* Norman: University of Oklahoma Press, 1984.

Death Runs Riot

Hoig, Stan. *The Peace Chiefs of the Cheyennes.* Norman: University of Oklahoma Press, 1980.

Lovejoy, Julia Louisa. "Letters of Julia Louisa Lovejoy." *Kansas Historical Quarterly* 11 (1942), 15 (1947), and 16 (1948).

Sanborn, Margaret. *Mark Twain: The Bachelor Years.* New York: Doubleday, 1990.

Twain, Mark. *Mark Twain's Letters.* Vol. 1 (1853–1866). Berkeley: University of California Press, 1989.

Utley, Robert M. *The Indian Frontier of the American West, 1846–1890.* Albuquerque: University of New Mexico Press, 1984.

Ward, Geoffrey C., with Ric Burns and Ken Burns. *The Civil War: An Illustrated History.* New York: Knopf, 1990.

The Grandest Enterprise Under God

Dary, David A. *The Buffalo Book: The Full Saga of the American Animal.* Athens, Ohio: Sage Books, 1974.

———. *Cowboy Culture: A Saga of Five Centuries.* Lawrence, Kansas: University Press of Kansas, 1981.

Haley, J. Evetts. *Charles Goodnight: Cowman and Plainsman.* Boston: Houghton Mifflin, 1936.

Mayer, Frank H., and Charles B. Roth. *The Buffalo Harvest.* Athens, Ohio: Sage Books, 1958.

West, Elliott. *Growing Up with the Country: Childhood on the Far Western Frontier.* Albuquerque: University of New Mexico Press, 1989.

Williams, John Hoyt. *A Great and Shining Road.* New York: Times Books, 1988.

Fight No More Forever

Hutton, Paul Andrew, editor. *The Custer Reader.* Lincoln: University of Nebraska Press, 1992.

Josephy, Alvin M., Jr. *The Nez Perce Indians and the Opening of the Northwest.* Lincoln: University of Nebraska Press, 1965.

Lavender, David. *Let Me Be Free: The Nez Perce Tragedy.* New York: Harper Collins, 1992.

Utley, Robert M. *The Lance and the Shield: The Life and Times of Sitting Bull.* New York: Henry Holt, 1993.

The Geography of Hope

Chen, Jack. *The Chinese of America.* New York: Harper & Row, 1980.

Emmons, David M. *Garden in the Grasslands: Boomer Literature of the Central Great Plains.* Lincoln: University of Nebraska Press, 1971.

Nelson, Howard J. *The Los Angeles Metropolis.* Dubuque: Kendall/Hunt, 1983.

Painter, Nell Irvine. *Exodusters: Black Migration to Kansas After Reconstruction.* New York: W. W. Norton, 1976.

Prucha, Francis Paul. *The Great Father: The United States Government and the American Indians.* Lincoln: University of Nebraska Press, 1984.

Russell, Don. *The Lives and Legends of Buffalo Bill.* Norman: University of Oklahoma Press, 1973.

One Sky Above Us

Emmons, David M. *The Butte Irish: Class and Ethnicity in an American Mining Town, 1875–1925.* Urbana: University of Illinois Press, 1990.

Gilman, Carolyn, and Mary Jane Schneider. *The Way to Independence: Memories of a Hidatsa Indian Family, 1840–1920.* St. Paul: Minnesota Historical Society Press, 1987.

Love, Barbara, and Frances Love Froidevaux, editors. *Lady's Choice: Ethel Waxham's Journals and Letters, 1905–1910.* Albuquerque: University of New Mexico Press, 1993.

Malone, Michael P. *The Battle for Butte.* Seattle: University of Washington Press, 1981.

Utley, Robert M. *The Lance and the Shield: The Life and Times of Sitting Bull.* New York: Henry Holt, 1993.

Waheenee. *Waheenee: An Indian Girl's Story.* 1927. Reprint, with a foreword by Jeffrey R. Hanson, Lincoln: University of Nebraska Press, 1981.

Wheeler, Keith. *The Townsmen.* New York: Time-Life Books, 1975.

Index

Photography Credits